This 2020 edition of *Voices from Behind the Mask* replaces the 2009 yellow edition. It also replaces the 1995 *The Geometry of Blue*.

In memory of **Ralph D. McGinnis** who co-founded Spare Change Press® and who opened my eyes to writing poetry with humor.

*

Spare Change Press® was started in 1979 by David McCoy and Ralph McGinnis. Regretfully, though, when McCoy transferred to Ashland University, McGinnis bowed out.

Voices from Behind the Mask:
Amended, Improved & Updated

by

David B. McCoy

Spare Change Press ®
Est. 1979

Voices from Behind the Mask: Amended, Improved & Updated

ISBN: 978-0-945568-69-8

Cover drawing by John Ziegler

Thanks to Mary Ann D'Aurelio and
Dr. Rhonda Baughman for all
their assistance.

Spare Change Press®
Est. 1979
Massillon, OH 44646
sparechangepress79@gmail.com

I admit that I am a minor poet.
I anticipate neither fortune nor fame.
I am confident, though, that one day
my poems will plague the world.

Although I know it's unfair
I reveal myself one mask at a time.

Stephen Dunn

The Discharge of Self

POETRY IS...

that butterfly you were assigned
to catch back in elementary school
once winter broke and spring emerged.

The moment you saw its flutter
of orange, off you ran with a cheesecloth
net fixed to a long wooden pole.

With your best ambitions, you raised the net far above
your head and came down
fast and hard and caught ... nothing.

An ache to catch that delicate
trickster settled in: soon you tried again
and again came down with nothing.

You then hid behind a bush and
waited for it to fly to you—quickly
snatching it right out of mid-air.

And what better way have I to
explain the process of my poetry
than through your not-too-simple task?

—words elusive, delicate, and
tricky until I net them with my pen
and arrange them into poems.

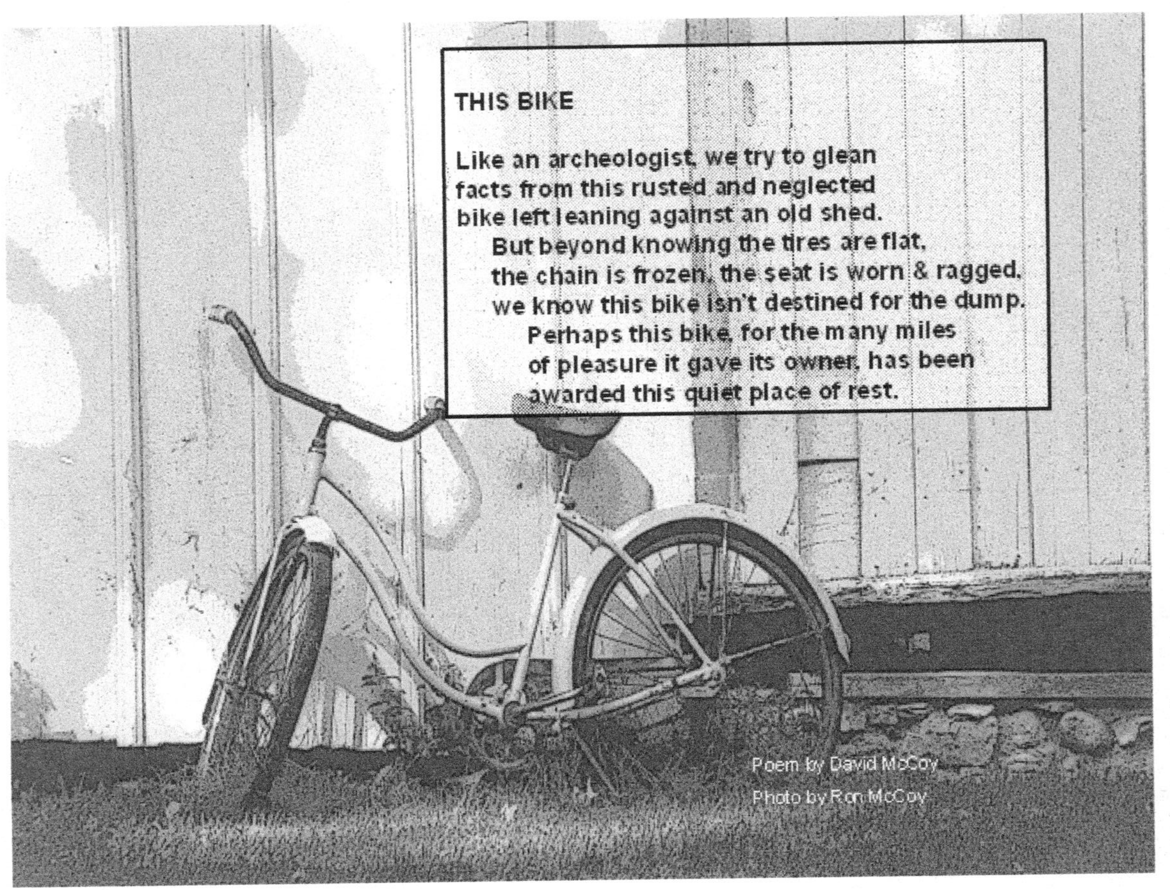
THIS BIKE

Like an archeologist, we try to glean
facts from this rusted and neglected
bike left leaning against an old shed.
But beyond knowing the tires are flat,
the chain is frozen, the seat is worn & ragged,
we know this bike isn't destined for the dump.
Perhaps this bike, for the many miles
of pleasure it gave its owner, has been
awarded this quiet place of rest.

Poem by David McCoy
Photo by Ron McCoy

THIS BIKE
Inspired by Ron McCoy's photograph

Like an archeologist, we try to glean
facts from this rusted and neglected
bike left leaning against an old shed.

But beyond knowing the tires are flat,
the chain is frozen, the seat is worn & ragged,
we know this bike isn't destined for the dump.

Perhaps this bike, for the many miles
of pleasure it gave its owner, has been
awarded this quiet place of rest.

WHAT LIT OUR LOVE

A year has passed
  since we arrived
at this, a place
  of love, which seems
as natural
  as the evening
    stars shining above.

And the great length
  of time it takes
for their brightness
  to reach thine eyes,
is the amount
  of time our love
    shall burn and shine.

And how our love
  did find its spark
I do not know,
  but wonder if
the force that lit
  the stars is, too,
    what lit our love.

GODDESS

After being together 2 1/2 years,
Jill asked a question that
stopped me dead in my tracks,
caused my knees to weaken
and my tongue to go numb:

Does this look all right?

My first reaction was to the danger of it,
and then to the overwhelming feeling
one surely felt when a Greek Goddess
decided to step down to this world
for a moment and become mortal.

Speechless, I took too long to answer.

BUTTERFLY

Those nights,
when you
wrap nearly
all the blanket
around yourself
like a caterpillar,
I half expect—
the next morning—
to be awakened
by a butterfly
resting on my chest.

FEW WORDS

Some evenings
few words
pass between us.

You may be
reading the paper
or a new book

and I may be
planning a new lesson
or writing a poem.

These are activities
we could do
in separate rooms

yet, the void
created when
we're apart

is too distracting.

SUGAR MAPLE

Spring (in regions where
stands of deciduous trees
dominate the landscape)
means trudging through
partially melted snow
to empty buckets
of cool clear sap
to be boiled down
into sweet golden syrup.

The daily necessity
of emptying buckets,
out of fear of losing
this precious liquid,
reflects my need
to see you daily.

FEEL LUCKY TODAY?
An Ohio Lottery slogan

They stream in,
one-after-another,
like ants returning
to the nest,
carrying a leaf
or piece of sand,
to buy
lottery tickets—
to play the odds,
knowing
"this ticket
is the winner."

I sort of feel
sorry for them.
Yes, I too
will march
like an ant
to our new home,
but the odds
are in my favor—
and I will
again
be a winner
as you walk
through our door.

LA GRANDE ODALISQUE
(Jean-Auguste-Dominque Ingres)

When I wake at three in the morning,
and see that you've pulled from your
body all the bed covers, I gaze upon
your beauty in much the same way
I admire Ingres's Odalisque, an idealized
female showing that "calm is the most
beautiful quality of the body."

TABASCO SAUCE

There's an old cowboy joke:

I've been married so long I'm on
my second bottle of Tabasco sauce.

In both of my previous marriages,
I made it to the second bottle,
and both marriages went bad.

I'll be damned if you think I'm
buying any more Tabasco sauce
heading into this third marriage.

STATE OF THE UNION, 2003

Tonight the President
    will deliver his
        State of the Union address,

but feeling
    quite content with
        our own state of union,

we will turn
    the radio off
        and go to bed.

BIRDING

Some men need hobbies
to save them from their wives.
Fishing and hunting
take too much effort.
In my family, drinking
at the local bar is suicide.
Fixing up old cars
has never appealed to me.
Stamp or coin collecting?
It's best to get out of the house.

Birding—that's a safe one;
you don't even need to learn
the names, the calls.
Just get out of the house,
take a flask, and return
home prattling on about
the blue jays, those damned
grackles, or the arrival of red-
winged black birds.

On mornings after an argument,
you can return and go on
for hours about a possible
pileated woodpecker sighting.
Truth is, in the end it doesn't
much matter: you both know
why you're really out there.

THE HAWK

Seeing a hawk dead on the road
is as shocking as a sudden bolt
of lightning on a calm spring evening.

With certainty, I can say it was
hit in pursuit of life it was about
to capture, or had already killed.

Its killing of rodents, rabbits, and
pheasants is as it should be—
as natural as the wind it rides.

But the death of a hawk by
an automobile or truck?
Why does this stir such pity?

I am relieved to know that crows will
soon encircle the corpse—ensuring,
once again, flight of an unlucky brother.

THE SINGING

I've heard
the stories
of this place.

A time before roads,
before houses,
before the plow.

A time when
the French
claimed this land,

and Indians
from surrounding tribes
gathered

to fish,
to powwow,
to trade prisoners.

I don't know
if any of it
is true,

but within the
steady rhythms
of Canton Drop Forge,

I swear, sometimes,
I can hear
ancient singing.

FAR NEIGHBOR

The land is more sacred
than it is beautiful.

A rain wraps itself once
about trees and stiffens.
It cracks when bent by wind.

I see my far neighbor
walking the stream as I.
Something lures us both here.

A strange old man. Seems to
know that Truth has no words.

THE PATH

The Buddhist monk who
practices walking meditation
would like this place...
Paths are wide and wind about
so as not to allow one
to see where he's been or
where he's going.

Plants that grow along the path's edge
are tall and keep one's wandering
attention focused:

First one foot moves, then the other.
The mind's eye follows each foot through
its levering,
its skimming flight,
its setting down.

The concentration centers
on the body's shifting weight,
the hanging hands,
the breath.

Sometimes, I too, practice this
form of meditation, asking myself
the same question the Chinese poet
Tu Fu asked himself on
one of his many long walks:

Why have I let an official career
steer me from my goal?

THE NIGHT

A moonless night:
only the stars,
a few planets,
dim arcs of light
from the refinery
from Belden
from Canton
from Massillon.

Before me,
complete blackness
until,
like a curtain,
the blackness lifts
to reveal
plants,
the trail,
steam rising from a pond.

I carry
in my pocket,
just in case,
a small flashlight
which,
to my surprise,
is unnecessary
even on
a moonless night.

GNAT SEQUENCE

Gnats
define
wind.

Gnats
levitate—
disappear.

Gnats
regroup—
drift.

Gnat
cloud
hovers.

Gnats
defy
rain.

Grant
draws
blood.

AUGUST 12th

This day is more than a cool day of summer.
It is the first true evidence of the earth's
positioning of the sun's rays towards the
Tropic of Capricorn. It is the signal
for trees to end their photosynthesis
and allow their leaves to usher autumn in
with a flare. It's when the earth passes
through the orbit of a now defunct comet,
and the scattering particles, no bigger
than a fist, alight the night sky.

This cool day means comfort in sleep.

THE HURT

My mother had the good sense
never to say it—
"This is going to hurt me more
then it's going to hurt you."
I never would have believed her,
nor should my son believe me
as I walk him to his room
for a needed "time-out."

Instead,
I leave him alone
to his own silent thoughts
and wait for him to emerge—
half gulping / half chanting—
"I'm sorry, I'm okay now."
And the hug at the end of the ordeal—
a sign of forgiveness; a way to say,
"God, this hurts."

MY UNCLE'S FORD EDSEL

In memory of Clarence Baker

I was too young to understand
the concepts of beauty or style,
but the day my uncle from
Meigs County, Ohio, drove up
in his new Ford Edsel, I knew
it was the work of angels.

A few years later when the whole
Edsel project turned into an
economic fiasco, I found myself
on the long road of doubt
as to God's reliability.

CRUISING, 1973

For Rhonda

It was our senior high school year.
Rhonda and I were cruising
back roads in Pennsylvania.
And though it was a dark,
moonless night in early winter,
I was brashly driving too fast.

The moment we flew over one
small knoll they were there—
standing stock still in front of the car—
their eyes glowing like candles:
Eight deer. I slammed on the brakes—
preventing an explosion of fur, muscle
and steel—preventing, perhaps,
our own deaths.

That was twenty years ago.
But from that night on,
like the dull ache some feel right
before the weather is about to change,
I have felt the movement of deer in my bones.

BURNING SPRINGS, W.Va., 1960

My grandparents,
before they got too up in years,
ran the big old Blair farm located
in the Little Kanawha River valley
just a piece up the road
from the Burning Springs "General"—
food store, post office, and
gas station all rolled into one.

Visiting them was to visit a foreign land:
A well for water stood next to the house;
kerosene lamps hung on the walls;
a heavy metal hand-iron, when not in use,
propped open the kitchen door; and chickens!
—kept in a coop out behind the house.

Grandma McCoy knew I loved chickens
and invited me one morning
to help her with the feeding.
Once inside the pen,
she handed me a tin can of feed
with instructions to "throw it out
in front of them and watch them eat it up."
And by God, in what a flurry of white they ate!

My aunts, too, standing together,
wearing long white aprons,
were enjoying themselves.
I also noticed they were pointing
in my direction— "yes, yes, that big bold
one trying to get all the food, let it be first."
"First," a signal to my grandmother
to ring her fingers around its neck,
carry it to a large wooden stump,

and cut off its head.

Instantly, it began jumping / running
around the pen—blood spurting everywhere:
a burning spring of blood
that caused my head to spin.

::

Sometimes, in one's life,
things connect and all is made clear.
This would be one of those times,
and no one expected me for dinner.

LEARNING TO FLY

From my patio I am watching
a fledgling bird learning to fly.

It reminds me of the first
intelligible thing I managed
to write in sixth grade—
some story about a guy
with a square head living
on the moon.

It was pathetic, I was pathetic,
yet my mother and teacher applied,
best they could without seeming
like phonies, positive reinforcement.

For a moment I flew—legs running
as fast as my flapping wings;
but many times thereafter
there would be stray dogs who
would nearly devour me.

This morning, watching
that fledgling bird, I am willing
to nail any dog who dares
enter our yard.

1997 PINEWOOD DERBY:
BOY SCOUT PACK 265

Brian used the provided pinewood block
to build his car, but the dangling roots
became entwined around the wheels.

Another boy used a Hershey's chocolate bar,
but it melted under the heat of the lights.

A third boy used a wedge of Swiss cheese,
but it wasn't very aerodynamic.

One boy named Mozart used ivory piano keys,
but it was as slow as weeping elephants.

The scout named "Johnny with Swift Feet"
built his car from the wind
and received the biggest trophy.

BANKS OF THE SEINE AT ARGENTEUIL

After Edouard Manet

How do you suppose
I should explain your death
to our grieving son
as we stand at an arm
of the great force
which swallowed you
and your ship whole?

At night, on his knees,
he has stopped asking God—
knowing that no matter
how hard he prays
you are not coming home.

Was it the maternal
rocking of waves and
steady hum of wind and sails
that lured you from the land?

Were we ever anything more
than foreign islands of life
in your vast briny world?

My year of mourning has passed,
but for his sake,
I shall continue to wear a chapeau
trimmed in black lace.

And, never take him to the sea.

FRIEZE OF DANCERS
After Edgar Degas

Degas painted
four dancers
preparing for
a performance

Degas painted
the dancers
sitting in
four chairs

Degas painted
the four dancers
lacing up
their slippers

Degas painted
one dancer
from four
points of view

GEORGE WASHINGTON CROSSING THE DELAWARE

(A poem in two voices)
After Emanuel Leutze

The hint of orange pekoe
that drifts through this wind
conjures thoughts of apple pie
she bakes with care.
        (*Row. Row.*)

Those hands, as warm and smooth
as fresh goat's milk, glides
one piping hot wedge from pan
to Canton ware.
        (*Row. Row.*)

The clank of forks on plates
resounds the door when
opened by her father—stern
in Puritan ways.
        (*Row. Row.*)

And when it closed, we knew
commitments to be soon fulfilled.
By summer's end.
Lord saw us wed.
        (*Row. Row.*)

Reared a Tory, father
was. Failing him in
war and marriage makes him sad
and bends him low.
        (*Row. Row.*)
Equally, I am sad
—but to reject

the Olive Branch leaves
only one alternative.
(*Row. Row.)*

So numb and stiff and raw
these hands have turned—
as much this oar as all its wood:
A burn of coals.
(*Row. Row.*)

Ahead a sheet of ice
appears to be afloat.
Does Washington not
see it? (*Row, soldier.*
Row. Row.)

FIRST IMPRESSION OF THE NUDE # 33

Patiently she waits:
standing there like a
Picasso of his Rose Period —
        thighs flapping inward
        with her head and torso
        slightly deformed.

She exerts her strength
in the way she mounts her hands
on those adolescently fat hips
        without losing the firmness
        of her breasts. Her smile seems
        to reveal our intimidation.

THE SLEEPING GYPSY
After Henri Rousseau

A gypsy
has fallen
into sleep
next to her
6-string lute
& carafe.

The moon is
full & round;
a few stars
speckle blue.
Hills in the
distance look
like...hills.

Some lion
keeps walking
into & out
of the scene,
half-hoping
to get in
the picture.

SUSANNA AND THE ELDERS

After Thomas Hart Benton

Never in her life had Susanna
revealed her flesh to the open air,

nor did she ever think she'd see the day
when there would be only a stream to bathe in;

but as her foot breaks through the flat surface
she is suddenly aware of her new reality.

Hardly less than lecherous voyeurs,
the elders Susanna has come to visit

look on from a distance as she slips into the stream,
telling themselves they've come to ensure her safety;

ashamed to admit their excitement—reminded
of their brides now stern and rough from work.

ON WALKING PAST THE VIETNAM MEMORIAL

Ascending from earth
with V-shaped wings spread wide,
carrying under your blackened feathers
reflections of Washington and Lincoln, you
are no mythical Phoenix rising from
smoldering ash to live again. Your
flight is of a higher destination—
to give some meaning and
honor to all those dead.

DAY OF THE DEAD

In response to 9/11/2001

While I am not Mexican,
this year I will celebrate
the Day of the Dead.
On a three-tiered altar,
I will place candles,
skeletons and skulls.
For those dead who return
I will serve chocolates, fruits,
Day of the Dead bread.
I will provide expensive tequila
and water—plenty of water so that
perhaps some will sing:

Here comes the water
down the slope
and my skull
is getting wet

There should be photographs
of the dead on my altar.
A picture for each departed.
But there are so many,
and from all over the country,
from all over the world.
So many dead.
So many photographs.
So many ghosts.

THE DIVINITY WITHIN

For Sash and Rekha Parbhoo

Those who follow one
of the four major religions of the Far East
greet one another with a slight bow
and hands pressed together
to symbolically say:
The divinity within me
greets the divinity within you.

While many differences exist between
Eastern and Western faiths as to
how to view God and pray,
within each one of us
radiates the Divine Spark.

And what better way to
affirm that common bond
than by embracing the peaceful practice of
greeting one other with raised hands
and a nod to say:
The divinity within me acknowledges
the divinity within you.

The four major religions: Hinduism, Buddhism, Confucianism, and Taoism.

RELIEF*

There's a young mildly retarded guy
who lives in our neighborhood.

He rides around in the afternoon on
his bike from the 1950s, wearing
headphones and carrying a transistor radio.

I enjoy seeing him, and almost envy him—
he always seems so happy.

Yet, I see him only in the world
he has somehow managed to create—
a world of music, lyrics, and
the rhythms of his bicycle.

It's ironic that I use rhythms of verse
to give my life meaning, to help me see,
while he uses rhythms to find relief
from a less than understanding world.

*This poem was written before the term "mentally retarded" was changed to "special needs."

FOR THE MENTALLY RETARDED*

So hard to understand why words won't flow—
his tongue and lips are stiff as frozen rope.
In class has mates a-laugh and watch him grope
for words too deep to whip the air he woes.
But tension (bottled tight) demands release
in time, and midst his patient vow to cope—
he yanks my hair and finds a solemn peace.

*This poem was written before the term "mentally retarded" was changed to "special needs."

LOVE IS A PLEASANT COUNTRY

Written for Marcia and Lester's wedding.
A variation on E. E. Cummings.

Sail down long and winding rivers,
and allow currents to be your guide.

Walk together across smooth running plains,
yet fear not to climb rugged mountains.

Be not discouraged by the falling of leaves,
in due time your tree will flourish again.

When called, scatter seeds for new life,
thereby assuring your posterity.

Be dedicated, honest, and sincere
to this, your country of love,

and freedom and growth
will be your rewards.

Yes, love is a pleasant country.

SQUASH

Huddles in the vegetable drawer,
secluded from all activity and light,
you timidly sit and wait—

(as did our cat the day we found him
at the pound near the back of his cage,
too weak and frightened
to venture out into the open).

June? July? When did you arrive?
Already it is January,
and yet you wait.
Paler now.
Softer.

I close the drawer.

The cat of this poem was named "Cloud" and lived 18 years.

SPRING HARVEST

Spring begins the same each year,
no matter how well we've
picked fields clean years prior.

The earth seems to send them up
through its thin skin of dirt

like...

        boils
                sweat
                        warts.

Each year before planting,
we walk behind carts
harvesting more rocks.

NURSES ARE LIFTING SPIRITS AND TOUCHING LIVES

Nurses are lifting spirits and touching lives
of those young and old, injured and ill,
helping patients back to health, to again thrive.

And though many are busy mothers and wives,
husbands and fathers working long hours,
nurses are lifting spirits and touching lives.

Often struggling with aches and pains derived
from rushing here and running there, nurses hesitate not in
helping patients back to health, to again thrive.

In what seems like an innate desire, I've
clearly seen the comfort they bring and the gift
nurses have in lifting spirits and touching lives.

Thus, in this week of May, it is our will
to pay tribute to those diligently
helping patients back to health, to again thrive—
to those nurses who are lifting spirits and touching lives.

THEME SONG
—for Wally Trace

Wally asks the new wide-eye busser
handing him a rack of wine glasses,
"What's your theme song?
  Everybody's got a theme song.
    What's yours?"

The busser is confused, not sure
  whether the question is actually
    directed toward him,
      and quickly ducks around the corner.

My pity for the new kid is replaced
  by my own groping for what I think
    would be my theme song.

Copeland's Fanfare for the Common Man?
(Granted, my ego's big, but not that big.)

Maybe that song by Blood, Sweet, & Tears
with the line:
  I can swear there ain't no Heaven
      but I pray there ain't no hell.

No...it's a Mellencamp tune:
  Your Life Is Now.

I like the ideas in the song—
teaching kids the truth,
            taking the high road,
    keeping our heads up above the clouds,

I like the line,
This is your time here
to do what you will do.

And it is: It's my life;
it's my time;
and I'm doing what I want to do.

VIGGO

6 February 2020

Tonight, a cosmic snowball of gasses, rocks, and dust is gracefully passing overhead as a brightly lit comet with a tail streaming across the sky for miles and miles.

And while it will soon fade from sight to continue its elongated orbit around the sun in the Kuiper Belt, it will never fade from our memories, our dreams, or our hearts.

The Sippo Lake Poems

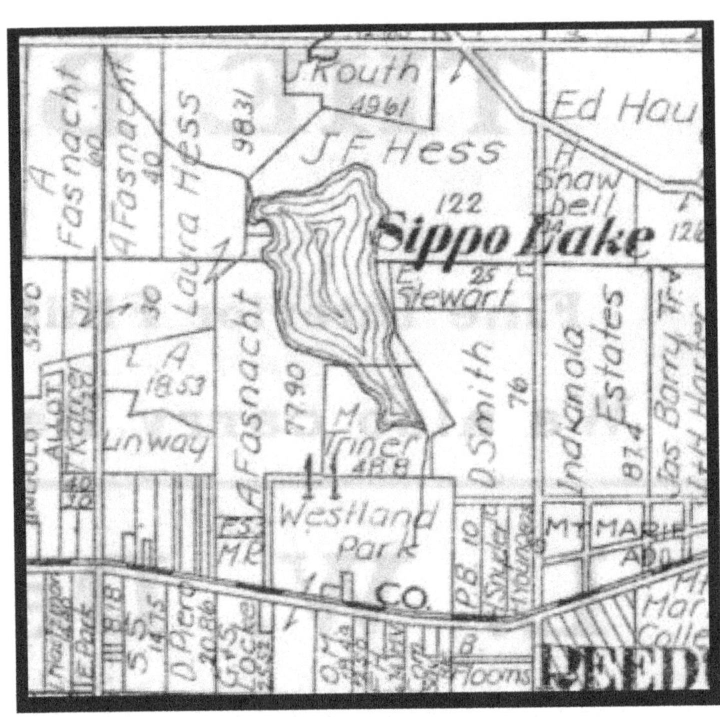
J. Routh
4961
J.F. Hess
122
Ed Hau
Sippo Lake
A Fasnacht
A Fasnacht
Laura Hess
9831
E. Stewart
25
A Fasnacht
77.90
Linway
M. Triner
48.8
D. Smith
76
Indianola Estates
87.4
Jas Barry Tr.
Westland Park
Ld CO.
MT MARIE

THE SIPPO LAKE POEMS

...poems are not
the point. Finding again the world,
that is the point...
Howard Nemerov

Sippo Lake was constructed in 1844, by James Duncan, founder of Massillon. A 300 feet dam stretched across Sippo Creek along today's Jackson Avenue/27th Street to create a power source for Mr. Duncan's mill. However, when the lake's water became stagnated, nearby residents complained of the smell and claimed mosquitos were spreading disease. When calls for the dam's removal failed, on February 23, 1848, saboteurs axed the pilings and the dam collapsed. A ten-foot high wave traveled at approximately 100 miles an hour towards downtown Massillon

The remaining section of the lake, and land surroundding it, were purchased in 1977 with a Community Development Block Grant because of its central location between two of Stark County's major cities. The lake is located between Canton and Massillon between Genoa Road on the west and Perry Drive on the east, and also between 12th Street on the north and Lincoln Way East on the south. It provides visitors with a variety of amenities, programs, and 202 acres of deciduous forest, wetlands, old fields, and mixed shrub areas.

THE KINGDOM

Not believing my new neighbor,
who told me one afternoon,

There's nothing but swamp
once you get past that thick
jumble of vines and briars,

I braved those vines,
those prickly plants,
the poison ivy

(indeed, vegetative moat)

and entered a kingdom
of solid ground which
I claimed as my own.

THE CAIRN

Cairn: a mound of stones piled up as a memorial or as a landmark

At my last place of residency,
I walked the rolling fields

and built with my son a
stone cairn several feet high.

Now it is time to
explore the 202-acre park

behind our new home—
knowing that instead of stone,

the cairn I will erect
will be built with words.

THE WALK

Leave behind the phone,
  the pager,
    the iPod.

Leave behind the mail,
  the magazines,
    the books.

Leave behind the TV,
  the computer,
    the Xbox.

Leave behind the car,
  the bicycle,
    the house.

Leave it all behind!
  Go grab an old hat,
    a strong walking stick,

and join me on my walk
  through the park.

THE ISLAND

After swimming through
the sea of dense brush
that surrounds this
northern section of the park,

and landing on what seems
a deserted, unpopulated island,
I begin to wonder if I am,
in fact, the first in generations
to tread on this soil.

While looking around,
I name those who have
walked here before me:
pioneers, Indians, mammoths.

This isolation of land,
in its vastness,
causes me to feel small,
and as I repeat the list
over and over again—

pioneers, Indians, mammoths,
pioneers, Indians, mammoths—

I begin to feel myself go invisible.

THE WIND

The wind...

The wind...

The wind pours out across the land with
the force of water thrown from a bucket.

Boughs break...

Leaves fly...

Stray paper tumbles...

Pollen and dust clouds form...

And the wind?

The wind...

The wind pours out across the land with
the force of water thrown from a bucket.

THE INTRUDER

I could hold them in one hand,
these rabbits on the path before me!

Still young, they do not fear anything
that is not an immediate threat

(and some will not learn quickly
enough to fear the circling shadow).

But for today, I am the sole
intruder into their world of play

that will be disrupted by a watchful
mother only if I get too close.

THE MOON

A full moon
casts pale shadows.

Only a few lone
leaves tumble down.

A hint of decay
fills the wind.

Already
we anticipate snow.

THE DUCKS

Tall brown
cotton-topped reeds
encircle this
adjacent pond.
Swimming
side-by-side
appear to be
the only two ducks
left in the park.

Too attracted
to one another,
they ignore
my passing.
Within a month,
this small pond
will be covered
with ice, forcing
them to the lake
and out into public.

Oh, what a pity
that would be.
They seem so
content together,
side by side,
and alone.

THE BARK

In the bark of trees
live some of the animals
that went before.

Many more live
within the rings,
but only those
in the bark
can you see,
can you touch.

Sometimes, I
like to rub my face
against the cool bark
to feel
their warmth or fur.

Sometimes, I
wrap my arms
around a tree
to feel their breathing.

When I die,
I wish to be
buried under
a young tree.

I, too, yearn
to make the journey
through roots
and xylem,
finding solace

within the bark
and rings.

THE TOY

Lake Sippo...was neutral ground where Indians would meet yearly to exchange prisoners.
The Perry High School Yearbook, the Clock, 1964

In one dream,
  I found on the trail
    a clay buzzer.

It belonged to a boy
  brought here for
    a prisoner exchange.

When he learned he now
  belonged to a new tribe,
    it fell from his hand,

and escaping from his lungs,
  the sad sound
    of the sighing wind.

A buzzer is a disk two to four inches in diameter with a strand twenty inches long doubled over and threaded through the two holes in the disk to be twirled. When properly spinning, a buzzer makes a sound similar to the sound of the wind sighing.

GRAY NOVEMBER

The color gray is what I think of
when November comes to mind

—that never-ending layer of
gray clouds; only birds void of

color rushing from one gray tree
to another; plants naked of leaves.

Don't bother with color film,
black and white will work just fine,

is what I tell our friends who plan
on taking photographs of the park.

NIGHTLY RITUAL

In the trees
east of where I live,
one can hear crows
preparing for evening.

It's a loud ordeal—
a warning of sorts,
or possibly
songs of reassurance.

As I enter their woods
voices cease;
only the flapping of wings
as they shuttle
from one branch to another...

In time,
I grow tired
of their nightly ritual
and move farther
along the path.

EN MASSE

Lifting up and above
one of several paths
hidden behind dense foliage—
the excited chatter of children
on a group field trip.

Distance makes what they
are saying as unintelligible
as the loud squawking of geese
flying—en masse—overhead.

As sudden as their talking
started, it stops. It's easy
to imagine an exasperated
group leader trying to regain
control of a half-dozen
crazed cub scouts.

12 MONTHS IN AND ROUND SIPPO LAKE

I / January

Along the bank, a rim of ice forms
at night only to melt under the sun.

This freezing and melting pattern
continues until we can't recall

the lake not being frozen over.
With a sigh of reluctance, snow falls.

The wind gives breath and form to white
swirling ghosts that whimsically dance

across the ice floor from west
to east and straight into oblivion.

II / February

This falling snow suffers
from multiple personalities.

Sometimes it is a fast moving
current of white water.

Sometimes it is a confused
swarm of gnats or mosquitoes.

Other times, it resembles a sky-full
of near-still hot air balloons.

When I reach out my hand in comfort,
it avoids me as if I were the

third rail powering an electric train.

A third rail is an extra rail used in some electric railways, instead of an overhead wire, for supplying power. It carries electricity at 750 volts, enough to cause very serious injuries.

III / March

While walking over to the lake
after looking at the hawks and owls,

Brian says, A week and three days
without a bit of snowfall

is a good indication that spring
is just around the corner.

I let his prediction go unanswered
knowing that winter is far from over,

but as we come across several robins,
he seems pleased by my continued silence.

IV / April

After a week of steady rain,
only a fool would be out here

hiking around on these trails which
feel more like damp sponges,

meaning my shoes will be caked
with mud by the time I return home.

Yet, here I am, welcoming back
my old friend, the warm spring air,

whose sudden appearance resembles
a door joyously swung open.

V / May

Poet T. S. Eliot famously wrote,
April is the cruelest month of all.

While I am not inclined
to agree with his assessment,

I am prepared to say,
May is the grandest month of all.

Plants are returning to glorious forms;
birds—native and migratory—dart

from here to there, and the sun
is wonderfully warm upon the face.

VI / June

Another night and early morning
of down-pouring rain.

The back yard is partially under
pools of standing water.

On higher, safer ground, two
young rabbits casually feed.

When their bodies are engulfed
by the tall unmowed grass—

with only their heads visible—
it gives the illusion of ducks

swimming in a sea of green.

VII / July

One afternoon while riding my
mountain bike on the park's trails,

I found myself engulfed by tall grasses
that nearly clogged my intended route.

Thicker and thicker, the grasses grew
until they opened up onto a rice paddy.

A long row of women and girls,
wearing Asian bamboo sun hats,

paused only momentarily from
their labor to watch me pass.

VIII / August

This 107 acres of park will never know
a harvest of melons or sweet corn;

it will never be a place folks come to
gather vegetables or pick strawberries;

and this land will never hold
a stand of fruit trees.

Only wild, untamed plant-life
will inhabit this place where

water takes refuge when clouds
release excess ballast from the sky.

IX / September

As long as I live here, September
will be occupied with this thought:

one would have to go back nearly
one hundred years to hear not one

airplane or helicopter in the sky.
For three days, Jill and I listened

and heard only leaves rustling
in the surrounding trees, joined only

by the varied calls of birds as they
traveled their own designated flight paths.

Sippo Park lies beneath a final approach path to the Akron-Canton Airport, as well as, beneath a common flight path of the Aultman Hospital helicopter.

X / October

And what is there not to cherish
about the month of October?

The countryside transforms
into a polychromatic display;

there is the continuous shower of leaves
which show great aptitude in riding the wind;

and there's a full moon that holds enough
legends to make a grown witch envious.

If I had my way, I'd have
a season-worth of October.

XI / November

The dark lump of fur that crosses
over from the park's thick growth

into our still-green backyard,
is one very large groundhog.

Snow mixed with rain is telling
it the time for hibernation is

fast approaching; thus only
the unrelenting steel-cold screams

of a jay can cause it to pause and
look up from its ravenous task.

The italicized from Thoreau's Journal, February 12, 1854

XII / December

Tall blond colored grasses that con-
gregate along Perception Trail

click and clatter in response
to biting December winds.

—Gone is the silky smooth
dancing and swaying of summer.

And even with my heaviest coat,
I, too, cannot escape these winds—

which goes a long way in
intensifying my pity for them.

The Clarity of Clouds

What is more appealing than an azure sky if not the docile clarity of a cloud?

Francis Ponge
A French poet

The fog is rising.

Emily Dickenson's last words

During my son's, Brian, eighth grade year, one enthusiastic parent thought it would be a keen idea for his small private school to have a baseball team. To field the team, all the seventh and eighth grade boys were recruited. Of course, Brian was excited by the prospect, despite never having played ANY organized sport.

The team members, by and large, understood their positions, but struggled with what to do with the ball if not caught for an out. And on the day of their first game, it rained, and it rained every game thereafter. After the first few games, I discovered the only way to endure the season was to pick out shapes and pictures in the clouds as they drift by.

Then around the fifth game, the clouds began to take on individual personalities. From a poetic perspective, this was a godsend which resulted in this The Clarity of Clouds collection of prose poetry. The prose poem, instead of having lines as verse poetry, is written in paragraphs. Consequently, it does not rhyme and seldom has meter.

Prose poems can be descriptions, anecdotal stories, the subjective exploration of objects or images, and yes, the personification of clouds.

CLOUD SEEDING

During the last half of the twentieth century, cloud seeding became all the rage. From airplanes, seeds of different farm crops were dropped into large billowing clouds, creating healthy, well-watered banks of agricultural crops in the sky.

Peas, corn, alfalfa, hay, soybeans all grew in abundance and floated across the sky like helium floats in the Macy's Thanksgiving Day Parade.

Assessing the economic potential they had been handed, clouds soon cornered the market on agricultural exports in North America.

This, of course, led Midwestern farmers to launch their long, but unsuccessful lobbying of Congress to have cloud seeding declared an environmental safety hazard.

WHEN MOMMY DIES

Daddy, when Mommy dies, I don't want her to go to heaven. I want her to go and live with the clouds. That way I can look out my window and see Mommy in the shape of the animals she reads me stories about.

TEARS

Great-Great Grandmother belonged to an Indian tribe out West. It is said that when she was sad, she would wipe her tears away with nearby clouds. When the clouds were tear-filled, she would release them to carry her tears to Mid-west farms in the form of mild, summer rains.

When Great-Great Grandmother had angry tears, caused by her drunken husband or foolish children, the clouds that were filled with these tears sometimes spawned tornadoes.

Great-Great Grandmother regretted the death and destruction caused by her anger, but knew it was not her place to break the cycle.

CLOUDS

One spring afternoon a father and his son venture outside to enjoy cloud formations.

After a few minutes, the son says, Look, Dad, two fingers touching. When they look around, they are sitting on ceiling-high scaffolding in the Sistine Chapel.

After a few minutes, the son says, Look, Dad, that cloud looks like an igloo and discovers they are members of a clan of Asians crossing the Bering Strait.

After a few minutes, the boy says, That cloud looks like the face of a Neanderthal, and they find themselves sitting around a circle of stones watching an awfully hairy man rub two sticks together.

Before his son has a chance to look up again, the father says, How about if we go inside; I'd hate to meet up with any dinosaurs.

THE DANCE

This year's flock of clouds over North America has been called home. They are to take part in the traditional dance called "The Hurricane." When this rite of passage is over, they will head north for the next round of lessons.

CLOUDSVILLE

In the Cloudsville Public Library, you will discover that the shelves contain books pertaining only to clouds: the psychology of clouds, the philosophy of clouds, clouds and religion, the statistics of clouds, the economics of clouds, the social welfare of clouds, the education of clouds, the language of clouds, the mathematics of clouds, the physics of clouds, clouds and the medical sciences, clouds and agriculture, clouds in architecture, clouds in paintings, photography and clouds, clouds in films, clouds in literature, and the history of clouds. And even in the glass bookcase behind the head librarian's desk, you will find a reserved collection entitled *The Secret Life of Clouds*.

TOP HAT CLOUDS

Near the end of the Top Hat Era of the nineteenth century, men rejected the traditional silk and beaver felt top hats for hats made from clouds. Unlike the static-shaped traditional top hats, cloud top hats were dynamic—their appearance always changing. Men of the arts preferred the wispy, feather-like style of the Cirrus Top Hat; middle class men preferred the Altocumulus Top Hat which appeared layered with a wavy demeanor, but the powerful business men preferred the Cumulus Top Hat with its noticeable vertical development appearing as a rising tower or skyscraper. A few oddballs in each city preferred the Funnel Cloud Top Hat, but they were seldom invited to social gatherings.

SIGN

After extensive research, it has been determined that the bank of billowing, feather-like clouds moving around the Midwest is comprised of evaporated chickens.

At first, it was thought to be a gathering of angels; then maybe a huddle of cherubs trying to keep warm.

The church has yet to release an official statement. They seem to be in some disagreement as to how this heavenly sign should be interpreted.

BOXCAR CLOUDS

During the years of the Dust Bowl, when a cloud couldn't be found for miles, hell for states, all the ranchers and cowboys boarded a one hundred boxcar train and headed east.

There they rounded up all the rain clouds the East had to offer and jam-packed them into the empty boxcars and returned West.

Once released, the thinking went, the broiling soil would cause the rain clouds to suddenly rise and release more than abundant moisture.

For as long as the trip took, the clouds held up pretty well. But when the doors to the boxcars were opened, the clouds refused to leave their new home and the Dust Bowl continued.

SCAB CLOUDS

The sheep of sleep have gone on strike. Oh, for the usual things: back pay, better feed, longer vacations. Parents are in a state of panic—they can't get their kids to sleep before midnight. To resolve the crisis, the National Parents' Association has begun to hire strike-breaking clouds which double as sheep jumping over white picket fences. While this seems to have pacified the children, negotiations appear to be in the doldrums.

BASEBALL

A boy, who is out playing baseball with his friends, smashes a high fly that disappears in the clouds.

Wanting to play some more ball, he climbs up into the cloud and begins his search.

All he finds is an arrow whose paint marks says that it belonged to an Indian named Crouching Bull.

Returning to Earth, he learns Crouching Bull has been dead over two-and-a-half centuries.

Grateful for having the arrow returned, members of Crouching Bull's family join in the search for the ball. Once found, they even hang around to watch a few innings.

The social worker briefly glanced through the folder labeled, “The Cloud family.” A mother, father, and two children, one boy, one girl.

When the social worker walked into the conference room, she found, well, four clouds. She had never treated clouds before.

Not knowing where to begin, she asked, “Now, what seems to be the problem?” It’s our son, Nadir, he’s always running off with those Tornado boys and tearing things up.

“Well, what do you think led to this behavior?” I’m afraid we’ve always been a bit lax, not just with Nadir, but also with our daughter Aurora. “I see. Continue.”

It all started when we lived out West and let Nadir play with the Chinook boys. By the time we got to Iowa, he was running with those Tornadoes.

“And when you tried keeping Nadir home, what happened?” He’d throw a tantrum—hurl things around, run out of the house.

“Mrs. Cloud, how would you describe your family?” Oh, I feel like a bunch of gypsies. My husband here just lays around all day; our son is out destroying or stealing things, and our daughter, well, she’s got one stormy personality.

“Right.”

MAGRITTE CLOUDS

On the eighth day, God grew tired of his cloudless sky and summons Rene Magritte to paint some clouds. Not since Michelangelo painted the Sistine Chapel had anyone been so honored, so Magritte painted a sky filled with loaves of bread.

"Great symbolism, Magritte," God said, "but don't you think you're being a bit premature?"

RAIN CLOUD

The old rain cloud has seen his share of wars: Burgoyne's failed march, the nine-month siege of Vicksburg, the awful years in Korea and Viet Nam.

His family looks after him now and doesn't mind if he sleeps all afternoon under the big willow tree.

On really hot days, his granddaughters take him tall, cool glasses of sweet tea.

IGOR CLOUD

Igor Cloud was schooled in classical music and is quite an accomplished harpist. Today, he no longer plays the harp because he is serving time in the Cloud Correctional Institution. Igor was convicted for disrupting outdoor country music festivals with deadly rain and hail. Secretly, he has broad support from the cloud community, but the head cloud magistrate is lead singer for *the Clouds-in-the-Sky* country music group.

TENNIS BALL CLOUD

It's another game of tennis. Well, not a game exactly—more a game of volleying the ball back and forth. We're not very good and spend a good bit of time chasing balls. After about 30 minutes, we've managed to hit all three balls over the fence. Neither one of us feels much like getting them so Brian says, "Why don't we use those low-flying clouds?" It's a thought that's never crossed my mind before, but what the heck, so I grab one. It's like hitting a cross between a beach ball and a balloon, and because it doesn't move quite as fast as a tennis ball, our game improves considerably. Our volley is now one long volley that continues well past sunset. At the point we can no longer see, we stuff the cloud into the can and head home. We leave our three lost balls for someone else to find.

EQUATION

Today, clouds are as scarce as straight guys in a gay bar. And yes, the sky is blue, but not like the blue skies out West which are a Boy-Scout-uniform blue—the type of uniform gay kids aren't allowed to wear.

I guess then the overall equation is about the same: there are no gay kids in blue Boy Scout uniforms and there are no clouds in this poem.

CIRCUS CLOUD

Most of the time people are content with passing their hand through me. Some like to take a karate chop to see me momentarily divided in half. Little girls, I like best—their tiny hands reach so tentatively for the smallest whiff. Teenaged boys are the worst with their spitting. If it were only gum, I wouldn't mind, but the tobacco spit repulses me. I prefer Northern states to Southern—that Southern humidity wreaks havoc on my sinuses. It's not the most romantic job, but considering where most clouds end up, it's pretty tolerable.

ADOLESCENT CLOUDS

Agony for adolescent clouds is to be stalled for days or weeks on end with no wind.

When the boredom becomes unbearable, especially over the Bible Belt or Eastern Europe, they like to get together and form the faces of religious leaders such as Christ, Mary, the Pope. Mother Theresa is a hit these days.

At night, they roll in laughter at the number of people they attract and wonder how long they can keep egging people on without getting into trouble.

When over Texas, they prefer to do Madalyn Murray O'Hare. It was so good once back during the 1970s, that they even got Phyllis Schlafly out to take a look.

THE SHEEP AND THE CLOUD

One day a sheep grazed too close to a barbed-wire fence which took the opportunity to take a piece of wool from the sheep.

The sheep, knowing what kind of fashion statement this missing patch of wool would make on the other sheep, devised a plan.

Waiting for the biggest, fluffiest cloud to float by, the sheep, in its best pathetic voice said, “Oh, kind cloud, would you please wipe the tears from my eyes caused by that wool-snatching fence?”

The cloud, in the classic style of Neville Chamberlain, soon discovered it had been tricked and was now permanently affixed to the sheep’s bare spot.

Not fully grasping its predicament, the cloud asked, “But who will now dry my tears?”

EVENING FOG: A metaphorical tale

Night was falling fast when Evening Fog drifted in. He was a prisoner of the wind and the blazing heat of the afternoon. His eyes were the color of denim blue skies, but you could see he was haunted by a deepening gloom.

The smell of things both living and dead mixed in the air, and thunder scattered crows from a nearby tree. And there was Evening Fog, hot and dusty, silently ushering evening into the lonely desert.

YOUNG CLAYTON CLOUD

Young Clayton Cloud was BORED out of his mind making the usual cloud formations: faces, animals, monuments, flowers, zodiac signs, mythological gods.

If he had to "make" something, he wanted it to be art, and modern art at that.

Clayton wanted to be Claes Oldenburg, or Henry Moore, or Robert Holmes. And if a flower, then an O'Keeffe flower; if a face, then a Cezanne face.

At the very least, he would be a Jim Dine robe.

All of the art mentioned is copyright-protected but can be found on the internet.

FIDEL CASTRO CLOUD

Despite Mafia hit men, military invasions, assassination attempts, radio and air-dropped propaganda, poisoned cigars, booby-trapped seashells, infected wet suits, one mother of a cloud in the shape of Fidel Castro keeps appearing off the Florida coast about an hour after sunrise.

Unlike his remarkable imitation of a piece of Limburger cheese during the Anita Hill witch hunt, Ted Kennedy insists that this cloud cannot continue to appear over US waters.

The CIA is being characteristically smug about the whole thing.

FOGHORN

There aren't many things clouds despise, but the foghorn is one of them. To clouds it appears as if man is attempting to take "the view from those who have as much right to it" as anyone else.

A five-second, deep throated blast every half minute throughout the night! Such arrogance from such late comers. Even before man crawled onto land, clouds were hovering around the coastlines of the world.

And the loneliness in those long, repeated groans: salt-faced men off deadly shoals, head—lands, and outcrops of rock; worried wives and daughters; sons yearning to sail off to false dreams.

CLOUD TERRORIST

For all the crap we daily pump into the atmosphere, civilization is faced with yet another terrorist: the cloud terrorist.

Looking very innocent with a calm appearance, it descends and engulfs the upper floors of skyscrapers.

Once most of a building is nothing more than a bank of white—in movement so imperceptible as to make icebergs envious—the cloud terrorist floats away with the upper floors snuggly concealed within its white mass.

Reports of widespread arrests of suspected clouds are beginning to emerge, but government officials refuse to confirm anything.

FLOUNDER CLOUDS

When I gaze up at cumulus clouds with their flat bottoms, I can't help but compare them to the southern flounder gliding along the bottom of the ocean.

You see, a flounder's body is compressed laterally and spends most of its life lying and swimming on its side. Even its eyes are on the "up" side of its head, looking up at the water's surface.

When I gaze up at cumulus clouds with their flat bottoms, I wonder if on their puffy, piled up-side, they have a mouth, a navel, eyes, ears, fins.

Several times, with a hook taped to an arrow and with a bow shot upwards I've tried to hook one with a bit of Danish Blue cheese, but have yet to get a bite.

OCTOBER CLOUD

The weather was harsh, which meant Lake Erie was treacherous. The soccer & field hockey fields I drove past on my way to college were covered by a cloud whiter than white and as thin as a communion host. My first thought? Snow. But it was early October, too early for snow this close to the lake. The cloud, the host, the vacillating puddle of white—as I neared the PE building—turned out to be a flock of sea gulls taking refuge.

DREAM CLOUD

In my dream I am presenting this manuscript to a publisher. As the publisher begins leafing through the pages, I notice the pages are no longer made of paper but of clouds—every kind of cloud imaginable. “I’m sorry,” he says, “we just did a cloud book last year and it didn’t sell worth a damn.”

THINGS WE NEED TO KNOW ABOUT CLOUDS
After Lila Zeiger

1. Have cloud stocks ever been considered to be included in the Dow Jones average?
2. Are clouds hermaphrodites?
3. Did Luke Howard (1772-1864), "The God-father of Clouds," love his wife as much as he loved clouds?
4. Did you ever notice how cooled barbecue briquettes look just like clouds?
5. Do clouds ever grow tired of following Eeyor around all day?
6. Do clouds self-segregate or are there cloud versions of Jim Crow?
7. Do clouds earn royalties every time someone uses the Windows cloud wallpaper?
8. What ever happened to the clouds that posed for O'Keeffe's Above the Clouds series?
9. Was that a cloud I heard singing, "I get no kicks from propane?"
10. Where do clouds bury their dead?
11. Does "You make me wet" mean the same to clouds as it does to beautiful women?
12. Do clouds resent being pushed around?
13. Do clouds have lucky numbers?
14. Do clouds accept contrails as distant cousins?

Howard, Luke (1772–1864) An English meteorologist who was the first person to devise a successful classification system for clouds, which he published in 1803 as a paper, 'On the Modifications of Clouds'.

Georgia O'Keeffe (1887–1986) was an American artist who painted nature in a way that showed how it made her feel.

Seeds of Change

SEEDS OF CHANGE

Seeds [of Change] is used to illustrate the changes that resulted when plants, animals, diseases, and people were exchanged between the Old and New Worlds as a result of Columbus's voyages of discovery. Scholars working on the Smithsonian's Seeds of Change project selected five seeds: disease, corn, sugar, potato, and the horse.

I listen to the splash of the Atlantic and Pacific and see Columbus land once more, over and over again.
—Joy Harjo

PART ONE

While Paleo-Indians tracked
large migrating beasts
across the frozen Bering Strait,
the harsh glacial environment
"cold filtered" from their germ pool
Old World "crowd diseases,"
creating for ten thousand years,
a pestilence-free world.

*   *   *

Having fed on nearly every
available human host in Europe,
the smallpox virus—
to ensure its propagation—
struck an unlikely alliance
with the previously uninfected
lower nobility of Castile,
and with a vengeance,
reintroduced itself to
the New World Natives.

*   *   *

Rolling on ahead of the conquistadors,
across the Antilles, to Cuba, to Mexico—
passing from one Indian to another—
the pox prowled the breadth of both continents,
leaving in its wake bodies inflamed with pustule
  sores,
shaken beliefs in gods, broken lines of succession,
and after the arrival of the conquistadors,
ninety percent of the native population decimated.

Corn

A. *Native Corn Song*

Before the sickness came,
before the Spaniards,
we made proper offerings to the God of Maize.

When the first green shoots appeared,
we went to the fields,
gathered some young ears and reeds,
covered them with our blood
and displayed them on our doors.

Once the maize was ripe,
the women
–with naked breasts and hair thrown loose–
swayed and twirled in spiritual rapture.

As soon as harvest time arrived,
the female chosen to represent
the mature maize was beheaded.
Her flesh was wrapped around the Maize Priest
who danced all night at the temple.

The God of Maize saw our reverence then;
He sees our dilemma now.
We thank you, God of Maize,
for your continued gifts.

B.

Raised by the Caribbean natives
and shipped back to Spain by Columbus,
carried to the Gold Coast by Portuguese
sailors on their way to the Spice Islands,
corn found a new and hospitable
environment similar to that
of its American homeland.

Astonished by its high yields
and abundance of calories,
the African people readily put aside
their sorghum and millet,
and for this, the God of Maize was
happy and the African population grew.

Sugar

With shoots of sugarcane on board
the ships of his second voyage,
Columbus had guessed right
that the subtropical climate and
Caribbean soil would support
a thriving sugarcane industry.

What no one could have predicted,
though, was that the Indian population
the Spanish had planned on using
to work their plantations would
be dropping dead from diseases.
So where could a large,
steady supply of slave labor be found?

In Africa, where the population
Was thriving on corn.

PART TWO

Potato

Because they were Catholics
in a kingdom struggling with
questions of religious tolerance,
had helped King James II
in his failed attempt at
reclaiming the British throne,
and was feared they would form
alliances with surrounding Catholic nations,

Irish Catholics were uprooted
and driven to the barren,
rain-soaked province of Connacht, *
where grain would not ripen,
and pastureland was too
inadequate to support livestock.
Through a war of starvation,
Protestant England hoped it
would be forever free of Irish Catholics.

But Connacht was where Basque
fisherman stopped to dry
their North Atlantic catch,
and stowed on board their ships
was a hardy tuber recently
brought from the New World—
a plant which thrived in cool
climates and proved to be
a rich source of nutrition.

Quickly learning to grow the new plant,
the Irish population jumped
600 percent in eighty years,

but their reliance on the potato was total.
Disaster struck in 1854 when a fungus,
arriving from America, caused
their plants to blacken and wither.

A million people died from starvation
or the diseases caused by starvation;
a million more boarded ships
and sailed to the land from where
the potato came, but most
stayed to tough it out, and
in the end Irish Catholicism survived.

*Connacht is one of the five ancient provinces of Ireland, lying in the western and northwestern areas of the island.

Horse Song

listen brothers to the song of my vision quest
watch warrior brothers the dance of my vision quest

a spirit-helper has revealed itself to me
my spirit-helper appeared as a painted ghost
my spirit-helper is the fleeting horse-spirit

listen brothers to the song of my vision quest
watch warrior brothers the dance of my vision quest

horse-spirit said it flew across the great water
horse-spirit said it escaped from the white warrior
horse-spirit said it missed the rich prairie grasses

listen brothers to the song of my vision quest
watch warrior brothers the dance of my vision quest

horse-spirit said it will help me steal fast horses
horse-spirit said it will guide me to buffalo
horse-spirit said it will protect me in battle

listen brothers to the song of my vision quest
watch warrior brothers the dance of my vision quest

Buffalo Neighbors

Buffalo Neighbors

Three Peculiar things about the Buffalo Neighbors poems

Until I was in my thirties, everywhere I lived my neighbors were borderline crazy. And in two cases, certifiably so. The crazy neighbor situation began on Abby Road in Elyria, Ohio and continued when we moved a mile or so to Bellfield Avenue. As one might expect, I lived with several oddballs while attending boarding school in Pennsylvania. The last odd couple lived above me in a large building in the town of Hartville.

Peace finally came when I moved to a nice home in Massillon, Ohio. On one side lived a sweet Italian couple and on the other was a Quaker Lady. But then it happened again. This time a wacko family moved *into my head* and stayed until I found a way of terminating their imagined existence. What you will read is only a small number of the poems and only those suitable for publication—they were hell-bent on driving me **nuts.**

Secondly, these poems, once published, moved people to ask if these neighbors were real. From a writer's point of view, it was very pleasing to be able to write something so believable.

THE WASH

Every Monday from my kitchen window, I watch the old woman next door wash her eight children in the old-time wringer washing machine. Once her children are clean, she attaches them by their hands to a clothesline to dry in the breeze. The children seemed to think it was all big fun during the warmer months, but this winter weather causes them to stiffen like boards.

As twilight approaches, she unpins her stiffened children and stacks one on top of the other in a wheelbarrow. With great effort, the old woman wheels her stack of kids to a cellar door and lugs them inside as one would surfboards. This might explain her need for all that firewood.

LAWN CHAIR

The eight kids next door love storms, not just summer-time, up-draft storms, but cold front storms that spawn tornadoes. Storms with lightning so powerful the fillings in their teeth rattle. At the height of storms, the kids rip off their clothes, grab long metal objects, and dance around an aluminum lawn chair in which one of them sits stark naked.

Today, during a hellacious storm, a big ass bolt of lightning hit the kid sitting in the aluminum lawn chair—causing her to vanish in a thunderous flash of white. The surviving brothers and sisters began jumping around in a frenzy that would have put sharks to shame.

By the time camera crews arrived, the kids had settled down enough to tell their mother what had happened. Staring at the smoldering chair, the old hag told the reporter, "I've heard of things going up in smoke before, but this is ridiculous."

NESTS

Nests start appearing in our tree, two and three at a time, shortly after the last leaves of November fall. I never see them being placed there, though I am sure it's the work of the kids next door.

The previous owner of our house is dead, so I don't know how long this ritual has been going on. By late November, there will be over 100 empty bird nests in our tree.

On mornings that I notice a few more nests have been added during the night, I recall how Indians placed tokens on the ceremonial grave of Jeremiah Johnson for each Brave he killed. I try to figure out whether it's something I am doing to earn all of these twig and grass trophies.

A month from now, a strong Arctic wind will knock all the nests to the ground. As I clean up the mess, I'll see them watching from their windows. While it would be a neighborly act, I'll not wave to them. I fear they might not wave back.

SNOW ANGELS

Today has been declared a snow day and the kids next door are lying flat on their backs in a large circle. With their legs spread wide, they touch their feet together—right foot touching left, left foot touching right—making a star-shaped flower. On some undetectable signal, they start waving their arms—making snow angels. After a while, their flower transforms into a dandelion gone to seed. When a gust of wind kicks up, they float up and over the partially frozen pond. This goes on all afternoon: flower, angels, dandelion, wind, flight. Only their mother—when she calls them in for dinner—can bring it to a stop.

SAP

The boy next door decided to spend the winter outside. So not to freeze and explode like a bottle left too long in an ice box, he dug down and grafted his ankles to the roots of a nearby maple tree—allowing the fluids of his body to be sucked into the tree's root system as temperatures dropped.

During the late days of winter when sap was again running, buds began appearing on his gloveless fingers, and buckets, nailed to the maple tree nearest him, filled with a dark, thick fluid.

When his brothers and sisters boiled down all of the collected sap, they found the dark, thick sap most tasteful.

MANNEQUINS

It was after the local department store closed that the stolen mannequins appeared at the edge of my neighbor's corn field. Each wore the uniform of an infamous military leader—Hitler, Tojo, Stalin, Mussolini, Franco—and stood in a knee-high mound of manure. I asked Ford if the mannequins were a form of protest, or maybe a variation on "Cadillac Farm" in Texas.

"Nope. At night they come alive and parade around my field—Hup...two...three... four—scaring the b'Jesus out of the crows who live in the woods over there."

Ford...

"Hell, you'd think it was a tight-shoes Saturday night the way they march that goose step. Only thing keepin' 'em from world domination is all that manure."

M-a-n-u-r-e?

"Ain't nobody gonna listen to a bunch of guys with shit on their feet."

ED SULLIVAN

For several years, the folks next door have been collecting black and white TVs. They place one in every window of their two-story house. All the TVs are set to the same program that plays 24 hours a day. At night, a gray haze engulfs their house. During the day, the house is surrounded by dozens of mesmerized kids from throughout the neighborhood. Community leaders have hired a cult deprogrammer to rescue their sons and daughters, but even he enjoys the show.

FABLES

Stories and fables that contain animals, especially Aesop's Fables, keep disappearing from my son's *Treasury of Literature for Children*. My son knows that I have no answers for him, but each night he asks, "Dad, what happened to 'The Hare and the Tortoise,' what happened to 'The Kite, the Frog, and the Mouse,' what happened to 'The Dog in the Manger?'"

Time passes and more fables vanish: "The Wolf and the Crane," "The Leopard and the Fox," "The Old Hound." Then one night, while reading one of the few remaining fables, we hear a great commotion next door. Pulling back the curtain, we see my neighbor erecting a large sign that reads, AESOP'S ZOO, and scattered around his yard, white-washed pens containing all the missing animals.

APRIL

A week ago, Saturday, Ford drove up in a full-size moving truck and set his family to the task of loading the contents of their home. It was a thing of beauty. Not only because those crazy-ass people would forever be out of our lives, but because their act of loading seemed to be an orchestrated dance.

All day—without exploding into the dysfunctional family we have come to know—they carried boxes, beds, bikes, couches, chairs, dressers, lamps, TVs, tables, that old wringer washing machine to the truck. "And that's the family," asked my wife, "who considers fist-fighting a form of bonding?"

Around supper time, Ford inched the loaded-down truck out of his drive and up the road. People throughout the allotment came out of their homes just to watch the truck disappear. For the first time in a half-generation, there was a feeling of calm returning to their lives.

But before we could reach our doors, we heard the truck returning. And when it came to a stop, the back of the truck flew open—releasing seven kids who started yelling, "April fools! April fools!"

BUFFALO TIME

The universe has reached the limit of its expansion and time is in a state of collapse. By noon, it's the 1870s and steam locomotives pull into town loaded down with buffalo hides. Believing that by morning we'll be experiencing the fourth Ice Age, the old man next door buys 500 hides and spends his early adulthood nailing them to his house.

PERSONA SEQUENCE

Persona who comes to visit has no invitation;
sleeps until noon and never makes the bed;
raids the refrigerator then drinks all the booze. After four
days it begins to smell of fish.

Psychoanalytical persona
parades around in the
shadows of the mind
draped in a black slip
quoting from
The Ego and the Id
by Sigmund Freud.

Hypochondriac persona
proudly wears its latest ailment
like a colored ribbon,
on a military uniform.

Orange persona gets pissed
at every college professor
who sends his freshmen off
to write stupid essays about
rotting oranges.

A Taoist persona
inhabits this house.

Just look around,
ten thousand things

all strewn about.

In the Taoist religion, 10,000 things refer to the multitude of daily distractions that cloud our minds and clutter our lives.

Glacier persona erodes
the human spirit by
gouging –
scraping –
and scouring its victims
until they are
little more than a heap
of terminal moraine.

Black hole persona grows fat
sucking the guilt of unspeakable
acts into its wide – swirling mouth.

Lettuce persona carries
the cries of dying Mexicans
in every head.

Stereotype persona
keeps saying
a Black or
a woman
can't be
elected president
in America,

knowing that
a Black or
a woman
won't be
elected president
in America,

as long as
it is allowed
to speak
its mind
in America.

Notions of Peculiar Intent

These poems are modeled after the Dada art form. "Dada was an art movement formed during the First World War in negative reaction to the horrors and folly of the war. The art, poetry, and performances produced by Dada artists were often satirical and nonsensical in nature" (www.tate.org.uk).

Second lives a life of seconds.

Second loses every race – every contest – every appointment by coming in second.

Second suffers from the middle child syndrome as a result of being born second.

Second always runs late and constantly hears himself say – *I'll be there in just a second.*

Second let his first wife slip away and is now married to his second.

Second always returns for seconds.

Second sometimes feels like sloppy seconds.

Second is always the one to yell out – I'll second that.

Second's curse continues in posterity with his second child being born on the second day of the second month of the second year of the new century...

Marching this year in the 2004 March of Dimes parade are ten floats.

Floats include:

the *Dime a Dozen* float with twelve cute little girls dressed up as dimes –

the *Can You Spare a Dime* float with 2 hobos –

the *Mercury Dime* float with the star athlete dressed as the winged messenger –

the *Dime Novel* float with the town librarian dressed as Laura Jean Libbey –

the *A Good Time for a Dime* float with Donald Duck –

the *Dime Bag* float with a Jerry Garcia look-alike –

the *Roosevelt Dime* float with – of course – Roosevelt –

the *One Thin Dime* float with a rather anorexic teen –

the *Stop On a Dime* float with Wiley Coyote on the edge of a cliff –

and *The Dime Store* float with the town's pharmacist dressed as a Norman Rockwell character...

My father is ill.

Ill with a type of cancer caused by asbestos dust whose harmful effects do not surface for 20 to 30 years.

Years of life are limited because there are only expensive short-term chemo treatments.

Treatments of chemical lawncare my father also pays good money for.

For his investment, his lawn is green and lush.

Lush as it is, his lawn must be mowed regularly, but he is too weak.

Weekly he calls and asks me to drive over and mow his grass.

Grass gets cut and back it grows.

Grows too my father's cancer and more orders are given for more chemo treatments.

Treatments of chemicals now regulate my father's life – and – mine...

Things from second-hand junk shops and dime stores – flea markets and antique shops – relics of the past – countless ordinary objects – trinkets – childhood treasures and mementos – Victorian bric-à-brac – scraps of paper – photographs – engravings – all carefully collected – labeled and stored in shoe boxes to retrieve later.

Retrieved later – instead of venturing out of his Queens NYC apartment– Joseph Cornell would explore his fantasies and dreams by creating small three-dimensional worlds within glass-fronted boxes.

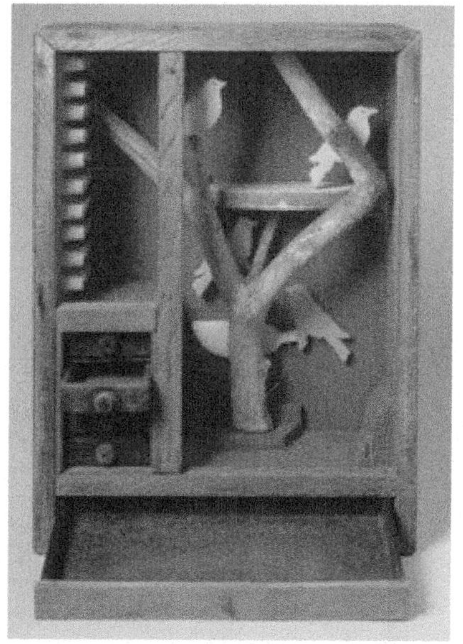

Boxes that reflected an entire universe in microcosm – yet always emphasizing harmony and the spirit.

Spirit of his work reflected Duchamp's ready-made art where an object [or objects] manufactured for some other purpose could be presented as a work of art.

Art – as practiced by Cornell – was to take readymade and illogical objects – which alone held no intrinsic value – and find their poetic connections.

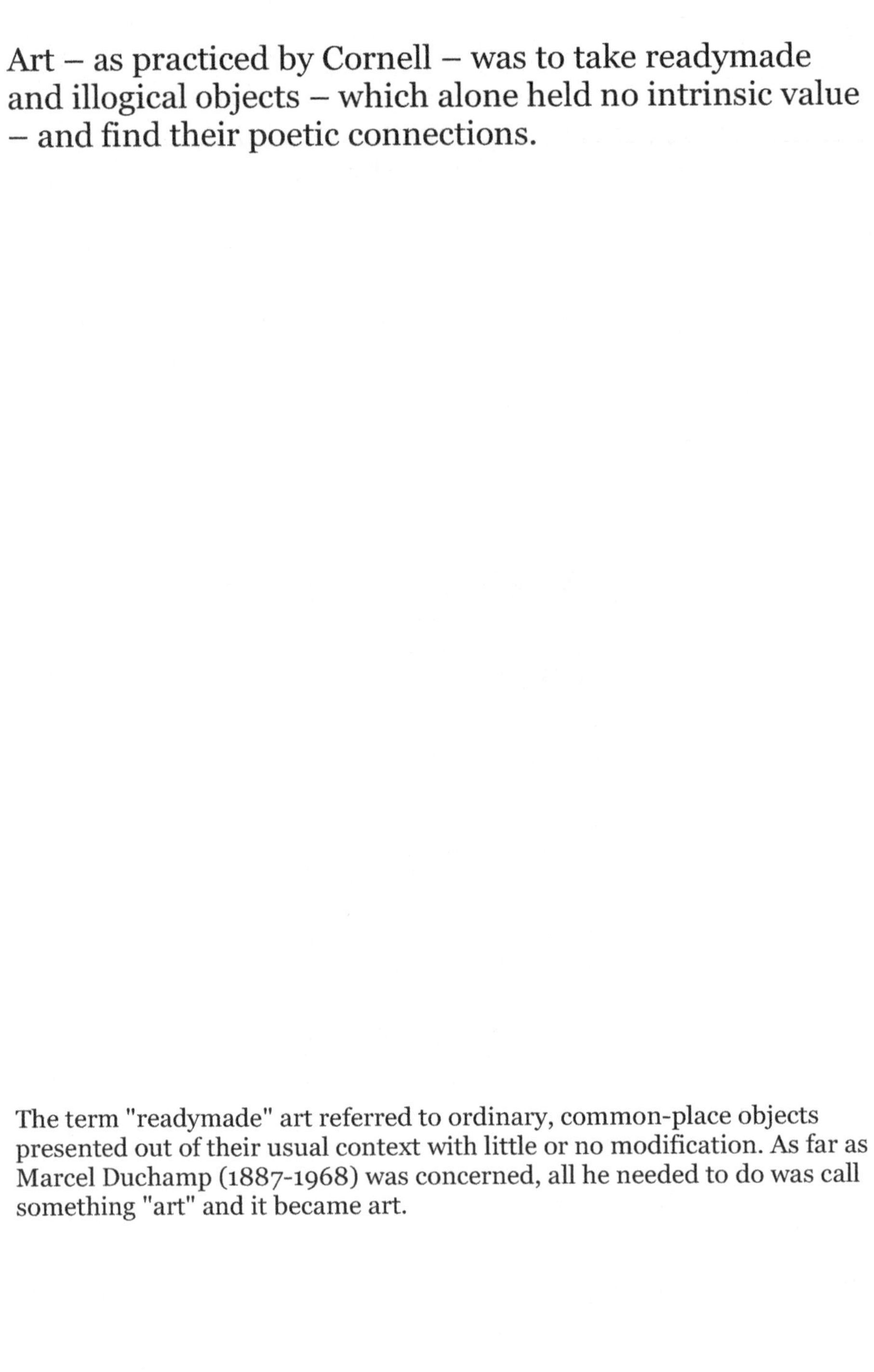

The term "readymade" art referred to ordinary, common-place objects presented out of their usual context with little or no modification. As far as Marcel Duchamp (1887-1968) was concerned, all he needed to do was call something "art" and it became art.

Oil runs thick
with spent human blood.

Blood-barges transport
crude to U.S. refineries.

Refineries thin the oil like
coumadin thins thick blood.

Blood-oil flows from refinery
to pump to our vehicles.

Vehicles guzzle the oil – the blood –
and spew spent souls from hot exhaust pipes.

wounded and dead children of Iraq
    encircle me –
wounded and dead children of Iraq
    stretch for as far as the eye can see –
wounded and dead children of Iraq
    reach all the way from this central
    point of Iraq to its borders –
wounded and dead children of Iraq
    cover the Middle East –
wounded and dead children of Iraq
    cover the land hemisphere –
wounded and dead children of Iraq
    cover the water hemisphere –
wounded and dead children of Iraq
    cover the earth –
wounded and dead children of Iraq
    fill my dreams and thoughts –
wounded and dead children of Iraq
    fill the universe and fly
    apart at the speed of light –
wounded and dead children of Iraq
    are becoming new planets and stars –
wounded and dead children of Iraq
    stretch for as far as the eye can see....

Mines – when used by armed forces – are to disable any person or vehicle that comes into contact with it by an explosion of fragments.

Fragments cause such injuries as the loss of limbs – abdominal, chest and spinal injuries – blindness – deafness – severe burns – psychological trauma – and death.

Death by landmines ranges from 15,000 to 20,000 people every year – with a third being children.

Children doing school reports will learn the countries that have yet to sign the 1997 Mine Ban Treaty include the three "axis of evil" nations of North Korea, Iraq and Iran – and – of course – the United States...

From making a stand for states' rights and the institution of slavery over one hundred and fifty years ago, came the first evidence that two separate societies – that of the agrarian south and of the industrial north – could not exist as one culture.

Cultures change and today we see the beginning of another struggle between the industrial minded and the service/information minded.

Mindless thinking will strive to conserve the fading industrial complex but the service/information transformation will occur—even if it requires another bloody bloodbath...

Applying truth and reasoning were obviously not standards deemed relevant by the boorish republican couple at a local restaurant who went on about how FDR was a communist – how JFK was a communist – how Johnson's war on poverty was the biggest socialist policy to hit this nation – that people put out of work just need to get off their asses and go out and find another job – that he is getting tired of paying taxes for services he'll never enjoy – *and if that was not enough* – **yelled out** – and 'you democrats love gays and lesbians' [– who of course are walking around serving people and pouring drinks behind the bar] – which prompts me to start waving my white napkin and declaring we give – **we give**.

Given the reaction of the people seated around the bar to his priggishness – and the waving of my napkin – you'd think he'd get the hint – well – you'd like to think that – wouldn't you...

Hitler will not be serving Pepper Beef Steak with Garlic-Cilantro Butter ~ South Seas Curried Beef over Jasmine Rice ~ Greek-Style Beef & Cheese Ravioli ~ Mediterranean Beef Steak-and-Salad Pizza ~ Tuscan Beef & Pesto Pasta because Hitler is a vegetarian.

Hitler will not be serving Pork Medallions with Vegetables ~ Pork with Parsnips and Pears ~ Grilled Pork with Melon-Tomato Tumble ~ Pork Chop 'n' Potato Dinner ~ Mustard-Glazed Ribs because Hitler is a vegetarian.

Hitler will not be serving Herbed Chicken with Spinach Stuffing ~ Chicken with Mustard Relish ~ Catalan Chicken Chowder ~ Turkish Chicken Thighs ~ Chicken with Artichokes because Hitler is a vegetarian.

Hitler will not be serving Cold Roasted Salmon ~ Browned-Butter Skate ~ Pesce Italiano ~ Crab and Swiss Strata ~ Grilled Swordfish with Tomato Chutney because Hitler is a vegetarian.

Hitler will not be serving Rack of Venison with Forest Mushrooms ~ Pheasant with Mustard Sauce ~ Simply Elegant Bear Steak and Rice ~ Grouse Breasts with Ham Sauce ~ Smothered Muskrat and Onions because Hitler is a vegetarian...

Vegetables and fruits – fresh and colorful on our plates – mask the miserable lives of migrant workers who are under paid for their 70 to 80 hours of work each week – exposed to harmful pesticides – are crowded into substandard housing – have substantially lower life expectancy rates – with children who do not attend schools and who suffer higher rates of chronic diseases than average American kids – all the while having to deal with bosses who cheat them out of hard-earned pay by charging exorbitant fees for food, housing, and transportation – but – hey – we are enjoying vegetables and fruits – fresh and colorful on our plates...

Worm Theater Productions will begin today at 2 PM EST – 1 PM CST and throughout the world in their respective time zones.

Zoning in won't be a problem because the Worm Theater Production staffers have embedded themselves into all the computers and internet providers throughout the world.

World-wide the Worm Theater Productions will – at the designated time – seize computers and transform monitors into short-circuit theaters and begin broadcasting.

Broadcasts the first week will include such programs as the Can-Can Dancers – Life Outside the Dog – the Night Crawlers Blues Band– and Making Sense of the Heavy Rain-Suicide Connection...

Character description of the author of this poem/journal reads as follows:

I don't spend much time on my appearance – I have moles in odd places and should probably clip my toenails more often – I'm as narcissistic and verbose as I am obsessive and introspective – I don't have syphilis – I have property, perfect pitch, culture, and credentials – I use Dial and Irish Spring soap and sleep with my feet outside of the covers – I am a Methodist however something tells me that Judaism has it right – I hate seafood – I hate fresh-water fish – I hate shellfish – I work for the government but it wasn't my original career goal – I'm behind on my rent and take medication to treat my depression – but – I have a mouthful of beautiful custom-made teeth...

Null Island Station

Quatrains are four-line stanzas of any type, rhyme, or meter. However, rhyme does appear in many poems, as does meter. Quatrains, in America, tend to be unrhymed and use free verse. Reflective of American translator of Chinese poems, Red Pine, and Walt Whitman, many lines in a poem line come to a full stop. By doing this, each line presents a full thought on which to build the poem.

In tenth and eleventh century Persia, poets composed Ruba'is, or quatrains, to voice criticism of fanatically imposed prohibitions, doctrine, and religious fanaticism. At other times, poets used quatrains to express personal feeling, beliefs, and doubts. (Peter Avery, 1981.)

SOME NOTES FOR THIS TEXT

Null Island is a fictional island in the Gulf of Guinea located where the equator crosses the prime meridian, at coordinates "Null,Null" or 0°N 0°E.

The Tang Dynasty was the golden age of classical Chinese poetry, while the Sung was a high point of Chinese painting.

The four major religions of the Far East are Hinduism, Buddhism, Confucianism, and Taoism. "The Tao" means, "The way of the universe."

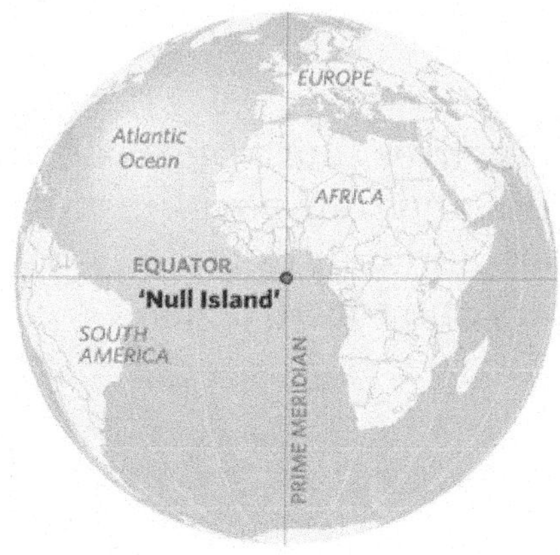

Two trains travel in opposite directions on the equator.
Two trains travel in opposite directions on the date line.
All will meet at the same moment at Null Island Station.
The collision will symbolize our nation's state of affairs.

The Quatrain family lives four houses down.
They have four girls and four boys.
They have four cats and four dogs.
They have four cars and four trucks.

I was driving home in a heavy downpour.
A quatrain tried to cross in front of me.
I ran it over with both front and back tires.
I took it home, but it was way beyond revising.

The Chinese poet Lin Pu never married—
never sought an official career.
With his wife—the plum—he taught
their children—the cranes—how to dance.

If this were the Tang or Sung Dynasty,
and I was at the peak of my career,
I would paint my poems on walls,
on rocks, and on my neighbor's damn fence.

Our new neighbors have erected
a five-foot stockade around their yard.
It reminds me of the Iron Curtain.
It reminds me of a chastity belt.

I write my poems on water.
I watch them flow downstream.
I always laugh when unsuspecting
fishermen get them tangled in their nets.

I am listening to a Symphony by Philip Glass.
I am listening to a Symphony by Philip Glass.
Glass is the composer of the symphony I am listening to.
I am listening to a Symphony by Philip Glass.

Philip Glass is an American composer and pianist. He is widely regarded as one of the most influential composers of the late 20th century. Glass's work has been associated with minimalism, being built up from repetitive phrases and shifting layers. Glass describes himself as a composer of "music with repetitive structures", which he has helped evolve stylistically.

My mother refuses to cross over.
She keeps showing up at holiday gatherings.
Not everyone realizes that she's dead.
That's why she steers clear of me.

⊕

Every day I read the obits and the classifieds.
What causes so many in their 50s to die?
Why are there so many burial plots for sale?
The mathematic possibilities simply don't add up.

Cremate my body when I die.
Scatter my ashes on deserts and beaches
where I may rejoin the earth's sand.
Require wine glassmakers to use *that* sand.

(After Omar Khayyam)

What an odd contradiction.
To pride oneself on striving
to earn a place in Heaven
while harboring such fears of death.

Heaven is no destination above.
Hell is no punishment below.
Heaven and hell are lived here and now—
each a reflection of our behavior and kindness.

The Chinese are a practical people.
They embrace the Tao, the Buddha, and Confucius.
I too am practical when need be
and cast aside the relentless wheel of rebirth.

To begin my path to selflessness
I am going to stay drunk many days
and gamble away all my wealth.
Only when I have nothing can I know the Tao.

(After poet Shams Maghrebi)

Every day for the last sixty years
the Buddhist monk spent mornings
raking water-smooth stones.
“This task frees me from the Self.”

Let me come back as the town oddball.
Let me go around talking to thin air.
Let me go around waving to phantom people.
Let me come back without a care in the world.

Yang Wan-Li wrote over 20,000 poems.
Today, nearly 4,000 still survive.
I can't begin to imagine the time he spent
  making all that needed ink and brushes.

(Poet Yang Wan-Li: 1124-1206)

As friends we build a bonfire.
Soon everyone is quietly staring.
Fire knows its seductive powers
and patiently awaits our arrival.

⊕

A bird flies through the open window.
I whack it with a killing blow.
After flailing a bit, it again takes to flight.
Everyone in the house is shocked silent.

Some unseen animal—a bird I guess—
  is calling out: chup-chup-chup-chup.
In my youth I would have gone investigating.
Now I just sit, waiting for it to fly to me.

Frequently Brother Crow brings me news.
Sometimes the news is good, sometimes it's bad.
Mostly I welcome his news whether good or bad,
except on Sunday mornings while reading the paper.

I am hiking down a deserted path.
In one hand I carry a rod and reel.
In my youth I always had such hopes.
These days, I don't even care if I get a bite.

⊕

A girl is out sunning herself.
Her skin is covered with glass.
If I reach out and touch her
she will shatter into a million pieces.

A week of dry and crisp weather.
Leaves are beginning to curl and fall.
Unlike undecipherable tea leaves
I understand these leaves quite well.

⊕

It's early October and 88 degrees,
with humidity as thick as smoke.
If this is Indian Summer, then
tribes must be on the war path.

Perhaps it is all due to climate.
Perhaps it reflects the mood of the nation.
But fall foliage lacks color this year—
going from green, to yellow, to brown.

⊕

The thought of it—being trapped
for two days beneath a dead man...
Considering all the cold weather exposure,
a photo in the local paper seems so minimal.

(Akron Beacon Journal, 1988.)

Could this be the result of the full moon?
A man asleep along the side of the road.
Another walking with a backpack and jug of water.
I can only image how my students will behave.

⊕

The sign on the corner was quite clear:
Post No Signs. Which goes to explain
why we are so amused when we see that
someone has planted over 50 NO! signs.

An old taildragger is flying around in circles.
Its engine reminds me of old WWI movies.
Several years ago all planes were grounded.
That's how the sky must have sounded before The War.

In response to 9/11/2001

Jeanie Marie likes the men
her father brings home for her.
Sometimes she laughs right out loud
when they rub between her legs.

At long last I have embraced Darwinism
knowing that our love will evolve into
a state of such perfection that we will be
the subject of all the scientific journals.

⊕

When I hear your voice, I am pleased.
When I touch your face, I am pleased.
When I kiss your lips, I am pleased.
When I hold you close, I am pleased.

Unlike the prophecies of Nostradamus,
my quatrains offer no predictions,
Instead I write about what I live
and see, with some personal opinions.

Trump says absentee voting is rigged.
Trump says early voting is rigged.
Trump now claims voting in person is rigged.
Trump lies to assure all voting is rigged.

Frost got the large apple tree this year.
There are no apples covering the ground.
Deer that grew up here look up and stare.
On November 3 we too will look up—but in prayer.

If they would rather die
by ignoring social distancing,
they had better do it, and
decrease the surplus population.

I admit that I am a minor poet.
I anticipate neither fortune nor fame.
I am confident, though, that one day
my poems will plague the world.

(after poet Cold Mountain)

The Day I threw An Eighth Grade Student Out My Second Story Classroom Window

THE DAY I THREW AN EIGHTH GRADE STUDENT OUT MY SECOND STORY CLASSROOM WINDOW

I was lecturing about William Penn and the Quakers when I looked over and saw Robert making a paper airplane. I walked over to his desk, took the partially created plane, and threw it into the trash.

“I don’t care if you choose not to take notes, but you’re not going to make paper airplanes.”

Robert then reached down, pulled out another sheet of paper from his three-ring binder, and began folding. “What are you doing?” I asked.

“I want to better understand the aerodynamics of flight.”

The dialog in this poem is almost word for word.

PROOF

On this last day of school,
I am stuck proctoring
a math exam with a room full
of eighth graders ready to bolt
like a pack of greyhounds,

and all I can think about
is taking the canoe out
to embrace what appears
to be proof that summer is here.

Yet, I know I would feel
a void minus your presence.

PARAGRAPHS

I am mid-way through
grading the fourth long essay
written this year
by my 8th grade students.

As always, the writing
is surprisingly good,
but I notice a lack of paragraphs
when there is a shift
from one topic to the next.

My assumption is that
students are hoarding
paragraphs for future use
on graduation exams,
or for jobs where
employers might value
educated workers.

Regardless of the reasons,
there is an absence of
paragraphs in the essays
my students have written,
and it's beginning to
grate on my nerves.

OUR CRAZY AUNT JANE

1.
By prismed windows
Crazy Jane sits
listening to
melodies of light.

2.
Janie doesn't frown anymore;
she's forgotten its purpose,
or found that frowning does no good.

3.
Some days Janie likes
the way she makes herself laugh.

DISTANT MOUNTAINS

It sounds brutal
to us today—
the way Spartans
took infants deemed
too sick and weak
from mothers to
   die lonely deaths.

Soon after your
conception, doctors
suggested tests
for Downs Syndrome,
and other defects,
should we want
   to abort the pregnancy.

As we listened,
I could see in
your mother's eyes
faint images
of women sobbing
at the base
   of distant mountains.

DELIVERY

On thinking about Brian's delivery

Piled five feet in front of me,
our annual order of firewood.
Until dusk, when too dark to see,
I will shuttle load after load
of wood down the hill and stack into
neatly packed, self-standing rows.
Over the winter, the long rows of wood
will slowly dwindle and reveal once
again rectangular patches of dirt.

When thinking of you, the reverse is true:
Instead of shrinking, your womb will slowly
grow larger and larger until one day
the child suddenly arrives.

FUR

I am at the zoo with my son
a few minutes past closing time.

We linger long enough to see
one of the tigers wander into a
small tunnel and remove its fur—
revealing an attractive girl in her mid-20s.

Dad, that tiger is fake!

"Son, adults play various roles in life.
Some are just better than others."

TWO JIMSON WEEDS

After Georgia O'Keeffe

Like a fool these many years
I've craned my neck toward
heavenly skies searching for
clues to the meaning of life,
when all the while I've held
the pathway in my very hand.

GIOTTO

A transparent image
of a bell with wings—

effortlessly soaring at
a forty-five-degree angle—

hovers above my son who
is sitting on the couch

eating green grapes
from an orange bowl.

I try to imagine
how Giotto would

paint such a scene in
his primary pastels

with all lines leading to
a thematic focal point.

But what would be the
thematic focal point?

The child? The grapes? No,
the transparent image

of the bird crashing through
a transparent piece of sand

to a higher / saintlier world.

CAIRN

Cairn: a mound of stones erected as a memorial or marker.

Each time we go for a walk in the field out behind our house, I add more rocks to the pile I started last summer. Politely, Brian stands to one side and watches—seldom asking any more what it is I am building. "Oh, just a pile of rocks," is what I say when he does ask, knowing he is too young to understand that rocks preserve memories.

Although the pile has grown in size, I can still identify events: Brian's birth, his baptism, that first step, that first sentence, the week in the hospital, learning to ride a bike, starting school, trips to Williamsburg.

When the pile grows too large, I will move down the trail and start a second, and continue to build until the next generation—Brian's children—can use my cairns to follow our path, to see his past.

MAYFLY

As a boy, I spent summers at a camp located on a small lake in Indiana. Every year near the end of July, the camp was covered with mayflies. I admired how they clung to the sides of cabins with their fragile see-though wings and long, stringy tails.

On one nature hike, we learned how the adult mayfly has a non-working mouth and dies soon after mating. The oldest kid from my cabin leaned over and said, "Far Out! Sex and death. The only two things in life that really count."

I was too young then not to believe him.

SPELL

Tired of old men allowing their dogs to poop on my lawn, I asked my gypsy friend to cast one of those "Stop dogs from pooping on your yard" spells. Now, when old men allow their dogs to poop on my lawn, the moment their dog's poop hits the grass, my lawn transforms into a brown gluey goo. Before the old geezers realize what has happened, their dogs are lost and they are left holding limp leathery straps.

BERMUDA: 1994

A Bermuda High has socked in the Midwest
and this combination of heat, humidity, and lingering
stench of cat urine, reminds me of old sweat socks left too
long in a gym locker.

The husband and wife team across the street—
wearing Bermuda shorts and white, knee-high socks—
take turns mowing their brown lawn. Long thin lines, left
by the wheels of their mower, record their progress.

From my side of the asphalt sea, I try to concentrate
on their diligence, but my thoughts drift and I am lost like
a schooner sailing through the Triangle.

WAY TOO DEEP

When I was younger
I went fishing a lot
but never caught
a damn thing, or
if I did, it was
only a twig or
hunk of moss.

After a few years
of that, I put away
my rod and reel
and even now lack
any desire to teach
my son to fish.

This same sense
of failure is what
I feel today when we
get on the topic of
our friend's marriage—

so leave me camped
on shore because
her problems run
way too deep for my
collection of lures.

LATE SUMMER

When worms webbed white gloves to branches of trees,
the horizon, too, was webbed white with mist.

When we did find courage enough to drive sticks through
sacks, only dead leaves remained.

The worms were gone.

MID-WINTER ICE STORM

The sound of my steps
punching through crusted snow
scatters birds with the force
of a small explosion.

And while I pose no threat,
they are reluctant to return
until I am safely gone
and lost from their memory.

CROWS

After Andrew Wyeth

Wyeth has nailed
to the side of his
pale-white woodshed,
like game left to age,
two large crows.

It is a message
crows understand.

CANTON DROP FORGE

All

Night

Long

A

Huge

Beast

With

Huge

Feet

Stomps

Up

And

Down

The

Land

LEAD POISONING, 1965

Aunt Martha is dead. Cars killed her.
Cars she knew as well as her neighbors.
Cars that were, in fact, owned by her neighbors.
Cars Aunt Martha waved to as they passed.
Cars she road to town and funerals in.
Cars with teenagers learning to drive.
Cars with tops down and radios blaring.
Cars with strangers stopping to ask directions.
Cars that nearly hit her as excited octogenarians waved.
Cars that pulled over and warmly idled next to her as she picked road-side berries.

DICTIONARY OF THREE BEAT TERMS
After Alberta Turner of Cleveland State

i) BEAT

Beat up
Beat down
Beat it out

* * *

I feel beat
I'm beat for cash
I'm beat to my socks

* * *

The beat goes on....
Industrialization, commercialization, standardization

Can you hear that beat?
Can you feel it?

They're beating the life out of us.
"I guess you might say we're a beat generation."

ii) COOL...

as in to the lower temperature
To lose the heat of excitement, of passion
To calm down
To take it easy
To cool one's heels
To be detached, aloof
To be calm, to be fresh
To be done well
To be very good
To be Hot!
To be Cool...

iii) DIG

Dig into dirt   flesh   one's past
Dig into dreams
Dig what they're telling you
'Cause, man, you're in a hole
You're in a rut
You're in over your head
Exhume yourself, baby!
Dig free of their nowhere shit and get it together.
Can you dig what I'm sayin'?

Donald Trump is Unfit to be President:

DONALD TRUMP IS UNFIT TO BE PRESIDENT: A FOUND POEM*

November 2016

Well we give them the election
That keeps filling our heads full of lies.

Can we trust in new directions
When their promises are in disguise?

Well someday the truth will catch up
I just hope it don't catch us all by surprise.

"Same Old Wine" by Jim Messina
Loggins & Messina, 1971

*Found poems take existing texts and refashion them, reorder them, and present them as poems. The literary equivalent of a collage, found poetry is often made from newspaper articles, street signs, graffiti, speeches, letters, or even other poems. A pure found poem consists exclusively of outside texts: the words of the poem remain as they were found, with few additions or omissions. Decisions of form, such as where to break a line, are left to the poet. (The Academy of American Poets.)

Donald Trump is unfit to be president because he…

Lied about opposing the war in Iraq.

Lied about why he couldn't release his taxes.

Lied about "thousands" at a Manhattan rally chanting, "We hate Muslims, we hate Blacks, we want our great country back."

Lied about his investments in Russia.

Lied about trying to make investment deals with Muammar Gaddafi.

Lied about his millions in outstanding loans to the Bank of China.

Lied about seeing thousands of Muslims in New Jersey celebrating 9/11.

Lied about Clinton wanting to get rid of the Second Amendment.

Lied about the Chicago police saying they could solve crime if there were tougher police tactics.

Donald Trump is unfit to be president because he is the one…

who said, To EVERYONE, including all **haters and losers**, HAPPY NEW YEAR.

Who said, I wish everyone, including the **haters and losers**, a very happy Easter!

Who said, I would like to wish everyone, including all **haters and losers** (of which, sadly, there are many) a truly happy and enjoyable Memorial Day!

Who said, Happy Father's Day to all, even the **haters and losers!**

Who said, Happy 4th of July to everyone, including the **haters and losers!**

Who said, I would like to extend my best wishes to all, even the **haters and losers,** on this special date, September 11th.

Who said, Happy Veterans Day to ALL, in particular to the **haters and losers** who have no idea how lucky they are!!! [As president-elect, Trump failed to attend a single Veterans Day commemoration. Loser.]

Who said, Happy Thanksgiving to all—even the **haters and losers!**

Who said, Sorry **haters and losers**, but my I.Q. is one of the highest—and you all know it! Please don't feel so stupid or insecure, it's not your fault,

Who said, Every time I speak of the **haters and losers** I do so with great love and affection. They cannot help the fact that they were born fucked up!

Donald Trump is unfit to be president because he claimed…

- President Obama doesn't have a clue
- Elizabeth Warren doesn't have a clue
- John Kasich doesn't have a clue
- Marco Rubio doesn't have a clue
- Karl Rove doesn't have a clue
- Republican candidates don't have a clue
- Chuck Hagel didn't have a clue
- Someone I just had to fire didn't have a clue
- Hillary Clinton has no clue
- Jeb Bush has no clue

Donald Trump is unfit to be president because he is the one who said…

Only very **stupid** people think that the United States is making good trade deals with Mexico.

Who said, Many Republicans support Trans-Pacific Partnership. They are **stupid**.

Who said, Right now 4,000 U.S. troops are **stupidly** heading to West Africa to help fight Ebola.

Who said, I'd bet the lawyers for the Central Park 5 are laughing at the **stupidity** of N.Y.C. when there was such a strong case against their clients.

Who said, Obama is, without question, the WORST EVER president. I predict he will now do something really bad and totally **stupid** to show manhood!

Who said, I believe that in addition to the 5 terrorist leaders President Obama gave up for Bergdahl, a great deal of CASH was also given. So **stupid!**

Who said, Do not allow our very **stupid** leaders to sign a deal that keeps us in Afghanistan through 2024—with all costs by U.S.A.

Who said, China is taking the oil from Iraq after we spent 1.5 trillion dollars and thousands of lives for their "freedom". Our leaders are so **stupid**!

Who said, Our very **stupidly** run Country better stop being so "politically correct" or we won't have a Country to run anymore!

Who said, South Korea must in some form pay for our help—the U.S. must stop being **stupid**!

Who said, Thirty thousand illegal immigrants with CRIMINAL RECORDS were released last year by our wonderful, though highly incompetent, government. So **stupid**!

Donald Trump is unfit to be president and fifty former G.O.P. National Security Officials point out…

He would put at risk our country's national security and well-being.

He lacks the character, values, and experience to be President.

He weakens U.S. moral authority as the leader of the free world.

He lacks basic knowledge about and belief in the U.S. Constitution, U.S. laws, and U.S. institutions, including religious tolerance, freedom of the press, and an independent judiciary.

He has demonstrated repeatedly that he has little understanding of America's vital national interests, its complex diplomatic challenges, its indispensable alliances, and the democratic values on which U.S. foreign policy must be based.

He persistently compliments our adversaries and threatens our allies and friends.

He has alarmed our closest allies with his erratic behavior.

He continues to display an alarming ignorance of basic facts of contemporary international politics.

He is unable or unwilling to separate truth from falsehood.

He lacks the temperament to be President.

Donald Trump is unfit to be president because he is the one who said…

There are too many "politically correct" **fools** in our country.

Who said, Can you believe this **fool**, Dr. Thomas Frieden of CDC, just stated, "Anyone with a fever should be asked if they have been in West Africa."

Who said, Prime Minister David Cameron is very **foolish** in giving so much money to build wind turbines which are destroying Scotland.

Who said, The Russians are playing a very smart game. In the meantime they are buying lots of time for Syria and making the U.S. look **foolish**.

Who said, For all of those **fools** that want to attack Syria, the U.S. has lost the vital element of surprise—so stupid—could be a disaster!

Who said, The Republicans look so weak and **foolish**—what the hell are they doing?

Who said, Look, when it comes to China, America better stop messing around. China sees us as a naive, gullible, **foolish.**

Who said, Iraq's government is treating us like **fools**. We should demand their oil.

Who said, Wow, what a day. So many **foolish** people that refuse to acknowledge the tremendous danger and uncertainty of certain people coming into U.S.

Who said, With Hillary and Obama, the terrorist attacks will only get worse. Politically correct **fools** won't even call it what it is - RADICAL ISLAM!

Donald Trump is unfit to be president because he claimed…

President Obama is **the worst** president in U.S. history.

Bill Clinton is **the worst** abuser of women in U.S. political history.

John Kasich is one of **the worst** presidential candidates in history.

George Pataki is one of **the worst** governors.

Eric Schneiderman is the nation's **worst** Attorney General.

The media attacks on me (Trump) are **the worst** in American political history.

Our foreign policy is **the worst** in U.S. history.

Our negotiators are **the worst** and dumbest.

NAFTA is **the worst** economic deal in U.S. history.

ObamaCare is one of **the worst** political disasters of all time.

Donald Trump is unfit to be president because he is the one who said…

Justice Ginsburg of the U.S. Supreme Court has embarrassed all by making very dumb political statements about me. Her mind is shot – resign.

Who said, Russia, if you're listening, I hope you're able to find the 30,000 emails that are missing. I think you will probably be rewarded mightily by our press.

Who said, [John McCain's] not a war hero. He's a war hero because he was captured. I like people who weren't captured.

Who said, Thousands and thousands of Muslims were cheering as the World Trade Center was coming down.

Who said, There is something on that birth certificate — maybe religion, maybe it says he's a Muslim, I don't know. Maybe he doesn't want that. Or, he may not have one.

Who said, Sen. Ted Cruz's father was involved in the assassination of President John F. Kennedy.

Who said, Khan's wife, Ghazala, if you look at her, she was standing there. She had nothing to say. She probably—maybe she wasn't allowed to have anything to say.

Who said, By the way, if she [Hillary] gets to pick her judges, nothing you can do, folks. Although the Second Amendment people—maybe there is, I don't know.

Who said, We have some bad hombres here and we're gonna get 'em out.

Who said, When people come back from war and combat and they see things that maybe a lot of the folks in this room have seen many times over and you're strong and you can handle it, but a lot of people can't handle it.

Who said, I think that her (Clinton) bodyguards should drop all weapons. They should disarm. Take their guns away, she doesn't want guns. Take them, let's see what happens to her. Take their guns away, OK. It will be very dangerous.

Donald Trump is unfit to be president and the following agree:

- Colin Powell, Former Secretary of State
- Condoleezza Rice, Former Secretary of State
- Michael Chertoff, United States Secretary of Homeland Security
- Robert Gates, United States Secretary of Defense
- John Negroponte, United States Ambassador to the United Nations
- Tom Ridge, United States Secretary of Homeland Security
- Robert Zoellick, United States Deputy Secretary of State
- George H. W. Bush, President of the United States
- George W. Bush, President of the United States
- Jimmy Carter, President of the United States

Donald Trump is unfit to be president because he is the one who said…

We have voters all over the country where they are not even citizens of the country and they are voting.

Who said, You have two and a half million or so that are registered in two states. That means they're voting twice.

Who said, Some of the voting is rigged. Everybody knows. Check out Philadelphia, Chicago, St. Louis.

Who said, Philadelphia is one that's mentioned. I think Romney got no votes and McCain got no votes. I mean, like no votes.

Who said, It's been reported that certain key Democratic polling locations in Clark County were kept open for hours and hours beyond closing time to bus and bring Democratic voters in. Folks, it's a rigged system.

Who said, Of course there is large scale voter fraud happening on and before election day. Why do Republican leaders deny what is going on?

Who said, The election is absolutely being rigged by the dishonest and distorted media pushing Crooked Hillary.

Who said, I hear these horror shows, and we have to make sure that this election is not stolen from us and is not taken away from us. And everybody knows what I'm talking about.

Who said, You've got to get everybody you know and you got to watch your polling booths, because I hear too many stories about Pennsylvania.

Who said, And I'm telling you, November 8, we'd better be careful, because that election is going to be rigged.

Donald Trump is unfit to be president and the following news organizations* agree:

- *New York Times*
- *Los Angeles Times*
- *New York Daily News*
- *Washington Post*
- *Houston Chronicle*
- *Arizona Republic*
- *Dallas Morning News*
- *San Francisco Chronicle*
- *San Diego Union-Tribune*
- *Sacramento Bee*
- *Baltimore Sun*
- *South Florida Sun-Sentinel*
- *Cincinnati Enquirer*
- *Akron Beacon Journal*
- *Charlotte Observer*
- *Tampa Bay Times*
- *Hartford Courant*
- *Columbus Dispatch*
- *Alabama Media Group*
- *USA Today*
- *Denver Post*
- *The Salt Lake Tribune*
- *The Des Moines Register*
- *The Omaha World-Herald*
- *Minneapolis Star Tribune*
- *Boston Globe*
- *Fort Worth Star Telegram*
- *Honolulu Star-Advertiser*
- *Kansas City Star*
- *Newsday (NY)*
- *Louisville Courier-Journal*
- *Miami Herald*
- *The Star-Ledger (NJ)*

- *Orlando Sentinel*
- *Philadelphia Inquirer*
- *St. Louis Post-Dispatch*
- *San Antonio Express-News*
- *San Jose Mercury News*
- *Seattle Times*
- *Chicago Tribune*
- *Detroit News*
- *Richmond Times-Dispatch*
- *The New Hampshire Union Leader*

Donald Trump is unfit to be president because he is the one who said…

26,000 unreported sexual assaults in the military—only 238 convictions. What did these geniuses expect when they put men & women together?

Who said, You know, it doesn't really matter what [the media] writes as long as you've got a young and beautiful piece of ass.

Who said, You could see there was blood coming out of her eyes, blood coming out of her wherever.

Who said, There's a lot of women out there that demand that the husband act like the wife and you know there's a lot of husbands that listen to that.

Who said, There has to be some form of punishment [for women getting an abortion].

Who said, "If Ivanka weren't my daughter, perhaps I'd be dating her."

Who said, Look at that face. Would anyone vote for that? Can you imagine that, the face of our next president?

Who said, Pregnancy is a wonderful thing for the woman, it's a wonderful thing for the husband, it's certainly an inconvenience for a business.

Who said, If Hillary Clinton can't satisfy her husband what makes her think she can satisfy America?

Who said, When you're a star they let you do it. You can do anything. Whatever you want. Grab them by the pussy, you can do anything.

Donald Trump is unfit to be president because…

The Donald does not rely heavily on advisers and does not read widely, if at all, preferring instead to watch cable television.

The Donald says he will bring a hell of a lot worse than waterboarding.

The Donald says he will unravel the Nuclear Non-Proliferation Treaty and encourage states in potential conflict zones to develop nuclear weapons.

The Donald says he will make the U.S. defense of its NATO allies against attack conditional on money, unraveling a primary stabilizing force on the European continent.

The Donald has no opinion or knowledge of the nuclear triad (the three pillars — strategic bombers, intercontinental ballistic missiles, and submarine launched ballistic missiles — of US nuclear forces).

The Donald insists global warming is an expensive hoax!

The Donald says he will "cancel the Paris Accord" on climate change and stop all payments of U.S. tax dollars to U.N. global-warming programs. Such an action would have severe and long-lasting consequences, not only on the climate of this planet we share, but on the credibility of the United States in honoring its word.

The Donald's economic world view eschews the notion of mutually beneficial arrangements.

The Donald has promised to pull the United States out of the North American Free Trade Agreement, abandon the Trans-Pacific Partnership, and withdraw from the World Trade Organization.

The Donald has repeatedly said that a trade war is nothing to be afraid of.

The Donald's administration [will] be an enormous shock to world politics (The Lowy Institute, 2016).

Donald Trump is unfit to be president because…
and the list goes on

& on
& on
& on
& on
&
∞

■

Postscript on why Donald Trump is unfit to be president:

On the night of November 6, 2012, when Trump thought Barack Obama would win the electoral college but lose the popular vote, Trump tweeted (only to go on to delete all but the last item):

The text:
[Barack Obama] lost the popular vote by a lot and won the election. We should have a revolution in this country!

The phony Electoral College made a laughingstock out of our nation. The loser won!

We can't let this happen. We should march on Washington and stop this travesty. Our nation is totally divided!

Let's fight like hell and stop this great and disgusting injustice!

The world is laughing at us.

More votes equals (sic) a loss...revolution!

This election is a total sham and a travesty. We are not a democracy!

Our country is now in serious and unprecedented trouble...like never before.

The Electoral College is a disaster for a democracy.

* * *

Trump said the election was rigged and he was not bound to honor the outcome of the vote, and neither are we—

HE IS NOT MY PRESIDENT.

Finis

*Compiled from *Wikipedia*

LAYERS: Two Essays Toward Understanding the Prose Poem

So I decided to cut loose and give emphasis to the imagination rather than to the line.

David Ignatow

One

Up until the twentieth century, poetry in the English language was dominated by strictly metered lines that rhymed. Because the meter specified a line's length, little attention had to be paid to line breaks. Therefore, once the writer determined the subject of the poem, it was his/ her job—while working within the confines of acceptable meter and rhyme—to hammer out a poem.

Finding both fixed meter and rhyme roadblocks in communicating ideas or emotions, poets abandoned end-rhyme and fixed meter in favor of free verse (meter more natural and more reflective of the poet's voice). In doing so, great attention was drawn to the use of line breaks.

Unlike metered verse, where the writer relies on a set number of feet to determine a line's length, a writer of free verse relies on the meaning or the emotion of words themselves. Other times, a line break reflects a half- or full-pause in a sentence. Some writers utilize a line break in such a way that it leads the reader's eyes to the next line. However, for most writers of free verse, the rationale of a line's length is much more arbitrary.

But regardless of whether a writer chooses to write metered verse or free verse, the "music" of the poem (created in part through rhyme, meter, and line breaks) is as important as the idea or intended image of the poem. It is this—the music/ image duality—the prose poet rejects. To the prose poet, the "music," brought into being through the manipulation of rhyme, meter, and line breaks, serves only as noise disrupting the image.

This is not to imply that prose poetry is absent of its own music—any good piece of literature is musical. But to prevent the disruption caused by rhyme, meter, and line breaks, the prose poet uses as his/her main unit of composition the sentence. "The sentence...while it does contain rhythmic patterns, has as its core a visual bias" (Stephen Fredman). This, then, allows the prose poet to squarely focus on the intended image.

Two

Appearing like a solitary out-crop of rock on the poetic landscape is the prose poem. Although Americans are at last embracing this form, little has been written about it. Hoping not to belittle the thing, I offer some generally accepted notions about the prose poem.

The prose poem is short, rarely more than a page or two in length.

Because the prose poem embraces the sentence, it is written as blocks of paragraphs.

Rhyme and meter virtually disappear or are hidden snugly within the text. What replaces rhyme and meter for some writers is a concentration on the syntax of the sentence.

Titles are brief, usually a single word relating to the story, object or image of the poem.

Although the repetition of verse is dropped, repetition of a word or phrase may be used to bind the text.

While some prose poems are descriptive, anecdotal stories, others lean toward the fable. But instead of teaching moral lessons, the stories turn fictitious to the point of becoming surrealistic.

At the center of many prose poems is an object or image. Here the author uses whatever means or devices necessary to explore its thickness. Other times, it may be a moving away from the object which drives the poem.

Exploring an object's duality is also a favorite with prose poets. For instance, the image or object described is so out of keeping with ordinary assumptions about it, the reader cannot keep from contrasting it with what is thought to be "normal." Sometimes, an image or object is presented in such a way as to highlight the differences between what "appears" to be with what, in fact, "is."

Because of the rebellious nature of the prose poem, the abandonment of even the broadest rules of meter and rhyme, and the adoption of the sentence, it is difficult to say anything too definitive about the form. Perhaps this aura of uncharted waters is fueling an interest in the prose poem. Whatever the cause, it is something limited only by one's imagination.

Where some of the poems first appeared.

Print publications:
Active Voice, Amber, Archer, Buckeye Country, Black River Review, Canto, Cleveland Review, Coventry Reader, Cokefish, Canvass, Conflict of Interest , Crystal Rainbow, Dreamscape, Daring Poetry Quarterly, Déjà vu (Kent State), Ear of Corn, Flights, GoodSAMARatin, Guts & Grace, Having Writ, Hungry Bear, Impetus, Live Writers, Lilliput, Masques, Modern Images, Promise You Press, Pteranodon, Pudding, Poetry in the Parks: 1989, Ptolemy, Plain Brown Wrapper, Samisdat, Singing Off Key, Spindrift, Solo Flyer, Sunday Independent, Ashland, Ky., Thirteen, Unity Church of Truth Newsletter, Vincent Brothers Review, Wurdz, Whiskey Island Magazine, Unfeigned Coffee Fiend.

Anthologies:
80 on the 80s: Ashland Poetry Press
Light Year '86: Bits Press, Case Western Reserve
Listening to the Birth of Crystals: England
To Have and To Hold: New York, NY
And What Rough Beast: Ashland Poetry Press
Above Us Only Sky: Incarnate Muse, CA
Four Crows on a Phone Line: Massillon, OH

Web publications:
iranian.com, bigtoereview, alongstoryshort, threecandles, a-pos-tro-phe, poetsagainstwar, thehissquarterly, autumnleaves, mamazine, redhandpress, ditchpoetry, deepcleveland, riverwalkjournal, poetrycemetery, theversemarauder, realeightview, colorwheeljournal, problemchildmagazine, writeoff, octavesmagazine, fullcirclemagazine, pinkmousepub, bluemoosepress, flaskfeview, ancientheartmagazine, zafusy, offcourse, thebluehouse, ahapoetry,

Bus Poem Projects:
RTA Cleveland, Ohio
SARTA Canton, Ohio

David B. McCoy earned his history teaching degree from Ashland University and his graduate degree from Kent State University. After teaching thirty-two years, David retired to write short books on a wide variety of topics. Before turning to non-fiction, he spent nearly 40 years studying and writing poetry.

Spare Change Press® Est. 1979

Short non-fiction, history-related publications

by David B. McCoy

Sparechangepress.weebly.com

www.amazon.com/David-B.-McCoy/e/B001K7WQHM

Made in the USA
Coppell, TX
23 July 2021

59372938R10142